"Wealth Within Reach : A Quick Guide to Personal Finance"

NrdWorks - Finance

INDEX:

- Strategies for improving current income
- Exploring additional income opportunities
- Developing skills to advance in your career

Chapter 8: Tactics for Tax Savings

- Understanding personal tax laws
- Optimizing tax deductions
- Efficient tax investments and plans

Chapter 9: Wealth Growth and Protection

- Growing your wealth over time
- Strategies to protect acquired wealth
- Diversifying investments

Chapter 10: Psychology of Personal Finances

- Understanding financial behavior
- Managing emotions and financial decisions
- Maintaining a positive mindset towards wealth

Chapter 11: Inheritance and Succession Planning

- Creating a succession plan
- Minimizing inheritance taxes
- Practical steps for ensuring a smooth wealth transition

Chapter 12: Maintaining a Healthy Long-Term Financial Situation

- Periodic review of personal finances
- Adapting financial strategy to life changes
- Continuous research and learning in the field of personal finances.

CHAPTER 1:

Introduction to Personal Wealth

As the sun rises on the horizon of a new day, so does the opportunity to transform one's financial life. We live in an era where access to wealth is at our fingertips, and this chapter will guide us through the fundamental principles to successfully navigate the world of personal finance.

"Wealth is the ability to fully experience life." - Henry David Thoreau

Throughout ancient times, wealth has been considered one of the most coveted goals of humanity. From ancient civilizations, where the accumulation of resources signified power, to the modern era, where individual prosperity is within reach for everyone, wealth has taken on various forms and meanings.

Today, personal wealth is not just about the amount of money one possesses but also the ability to wisely manage financial resources to create a fulfilling life. It is a journey that requires awareness, planning, and action.

Throughout history, individuals like Benjamin Franklin emphasized the importance of personal financial management. Franklin, with his famous saying, "A penny saved is a penny earned," highlighted the value of saving as the foundation for building wealth.

During the Great Depression of the 1930s, U.S. President Franklin D. Roosevelt introduced the New Deal, a package of economic programs aimed at stimulating employment and stabilizing the economy. This period underscored the significance of economic policies in the lives of ordinary people.

Steve Jobs, the visionary co-founder of Apple, emphasized how his experience of financial failure and success shaped him. He stated, "I've been rich and I've been poor. Rich is better." Jobs highlighted the importance of investing in one's mind and expertise, as well as material possessions.

The Path to Personal Wealth:

The journey begins by understanding that wealth is a combination of income, savings, and smart investments. It's a balance between living in the present and planning for the future. Throughout this book, we will explore tools and strategies to build a solid financial foundation, inspired by the words of those who came before us and shaped how we perceive wealth today.

"Don't let money control you. Control money." - Jack Welch

With this spirit of financial control and awareness, we embark on our journey toward accessible wealth.

Definition of Personal Wealth

Personal wealth goes beyond the mere accumulation of money; it is a concept that encompasses the entire sphere of individual prosperity. While some may identify it with a substantial bank balance or ownership of luxury goods, its true essence lies in the ability to wisely utilize available resources to create a satisfying life in every aspect.

Wealth as Quality of Life:

Personal wealth is not solely measured in currency but in the quality of life an individual can experience. It includes aspects such as health, relationships, personal development, and professional satisfaction. A truly rich individual is one who finds a harmonious balance between the material and immaterial aspects of life.

Temporal Dimension:

Personal wealth takes into account the temporal dimension,

considering both the present and the future. It is not just about the immediate fulfillment of desires but also the ability to plan intelligently to ensure long-term financial stability. A prudent approach to financial management reflects awareness of personal growth over time.

Financial Self-Determination:

Being personally wealthy means being masters of one's financial destiny. It involves taking control of one's economic situation, understanding fundamental financial principles, and making conscious decisions to achieve financial goals. Financial self-determination also entails the ability to adapt to financial challenges and learn from one's mistakes.

"Wealth is the ability to dream and see dreams turn into reality." - Aliko Dangote

Key Elements of Personal Wealth:

1. Financial Resources: Naturally, money plays a central role, but wise management of financial resources is crucial for lasting wealth.

2. Personal Satisfaction: Personal wealth is also tied to the satisfaction derived from achieving goals, pursuing passions, and living a meaningful life.

3. Personal Development: Personal growth is a fundamental pillar of wealth. Investing in education, skills, and personal well-being contributes to individual enrichment.

4. Healthy Relationships: Meaningful connections and strong relationships are essential for personal wealth. A broad support network contributes to emotional well-being and overall prosperity.

In summary, personal wealth is a combination of financial well-being, personal satisfaction, and individual growth. Throughout this book, we will explore practical strategies to develop each aspect of personal wealth, creating a solid foundation for a fulfilling and prosperous life.

Importance of Managing
Personal Finances

Managing personal finances is a crucial aspect of individual economic well-being. It's not just about tracking income and expenses but cultivating financial awareness to make informed decisions and build a solid foundation for the future. Let's explore why managing personal finances is so important:

1. Financial Stability:
   - Personal finance management is the cornerstone of economic stability. Planning and following a budget ensure that income is sufficient to cover expenses, thereby avoiding precarious financial situations.

2. Prevention of Excessive Debt:
   - Prudent financial management helps avoid resorting to excessive debt. Uncontrolled debt can become a chain that limits financial possibilities and hinders wealth-building.

3. Achievement of Financial Goals:
   - Financial planning allows for setting clear financial goals, such as saving for children's education, buying a home, or retirement. Effective financial management is the key to achieving such goals.

4. Creation of an Emergency Fund:
   - Life is unpredictable, and an emergency fund is essential to cope with unforeseen expenses like medical care or job loss. Conscious financial management allows for building and maintaining a robust emergency fund.

5. Intelligent Investments:
   - Effective financial management opens the door to intelligent investments. Targeted investments can grow wealth over time and contribute to realizing long-term financial dreams.

6. Reduction of Financial Stress:
   - Inability to manage finances can lead to increasing financial stress. Financial awareness and planning help reduce anxiety related to financial matters, thereby improving overall quality of life.

7. Awareness of Financial Opportunities:

- Financial management is not only about saving but also awareness of financial opportunities. Being informed about investments, interest rates, and tax strategies paves the way for smarter financial decisions.

"The management of finances is not just about what we do with our money, but what we do with our lives." - Dave Ramsey

"The best way to predict the future is to create it." - Peter Drucker

Managing personal finances is an investment in oneself and one's future. It is a demonstration of personal responsibility and a path toward achieving a financially fulfilling life. Throughout this book, we will explore best practices for wisely managing personal finances, thus laying the groundwork for lasting prosperity.

Short and Long-Term Financial Goals

The key to effective financial management lies in defining clear and realistic financial goals, both short and long-term. Goals act as a compass in navigating the financial journey, guiding daily decisions and directing efforts toward achieving meaningful milestones. Let's explore why defining financial goals is so crucial:

1. Clarity and Focus:

- Financial goals provide a clear direction for managing personal finances. They offer a sense of focus and determination, steering clear of impulsive financial decisions and channeling efforts toward specific objectives.

2. Expense Control:

- Financial goals serve as a mechanism for controlling expenses. With a clear vision of what you want to achieve, you are more likely to assess priorities and avoid unnecessary expenses that could hinder progress toward the goal.

3. Structured Saving:

- Defining financial goals helps structure savings. For example, setting a monthly savings goal for a trip, additional education, or creating an emergency fund establishes a tangible action plan.

4. Motivation and Commitment:

- Financial goals act as a source of motivation. Awareness of desired outcomes makes individuals more inclined to actively engage in financial management. The prospect of achieving challenging goals can be a powerful motivational force.

5. Personal Satisfaction:

- Achieving financial goals provides deep personal satisfaction. Progressing toward both small and large goals contributes to building a sense of accomplishment and self-efficacy.

6. Long-Term Financial Security:

- Long-term financial goals, such as retirement savings or building an investment portfolio, contribute to ensuring financial security over the years. Planning ahead for the future helps mitigate the risk of financial difficulties in later stages of life.

7. Adaptation to Life Changes:

- By defining financial goals, individuals are better prepared to face life changes, such as job transitions, unexpected expenses, or new personal milestones. Flexibility in adapting goals to changing circumstances is crucial for long-term financial success.

"A goal without a plan is just a wish." - Antoine de Saint-Exupéry

Defining financial goals is a fundamental step in building a financially fulfilling life. Throughout this book, we will explore practical strategies for establishing, pursuing, and achieving short and long-term financial goals, thereby creating a solid foundation for personal prosperity.

CHAPTER 2:

Creating an Effective Budget

The concept of budgeting has deep roots in financial history and remains an essential pillar for effective financial management. Today, in the present, budgeting is more relevant than ever to help individuals chart their path to financial success.

The concept of budgeting can be traced back to the basic principles of financial administration in ancient times. Civilizations like the ancient Romans were known for using financial records to monitor income and expenses. Over time, financial management has evolved, with Dave Ramsey's famous "Zero-Based Budget" gaining popularity in the 21st century, promoting the concept of allocating every dollar to a specific purpose.

The Importance of Budgeting Today:

1. Expense Control:
   - An effective budget is a key tool for expense control. Identifying spending categories and allocating funds reasonably helps avoid waste and maintain a balance between income and expenses.

2. Financial Planning:
   - Budgeting is a form of financial planning. It allows for setting realistic financial goals, allocating resources appropriately, and monitoring progress over time.

3. Saving and Investments:

- With a well-structured budget, it's possible to identify areas for saving and allocate resources for investments. This contributes to wealth growth over time.

4. Debt Prevention:

- Budgeting helps prevent excessive reliance on debt. Regularly monitoring finances enables the identification of potential financial issues and the adoption of preventive measures.

5. Adaptability to Changes:

- A flexible budget adapts to life variations, such as changes in income, new expenses, or unforeseen circumstances. This flexibility is crucial for addressing the ever-changing dynamics of daily life.

Practical Examples:

Let's assume a monthly income of 3000 euros. Creating a budget might involve allocating this sum into different categories:
  - Housing: 1000 euros
  - Food: 300 euros
  - Transportation: 150 euros
  - Entertainment: 200 euros
  - Savings: 200 euros
  - Remaining for miscellaneous expenses: 1150 euros

This example illustrates how a budget assigns each euro to a specific category, promoting a fair distribution of resources.

"The budget is a form of financial expression. A person can say anything they want with their budget." - George S. Clason

Budgeting is a key practice to maintain a healthy financial control in the present and build a solid foundation for the future. In the next chapter, we will explore practical strategies for creating and effectively managing a personalized budget.

The Importance of Budgeting

Budgeting serves as the cornerstone of personal financial management. Its significance lies in its inherent ability to provide a detailed map of personal finances, offering invaluable guidance for those aspiring to long-term financial stability. Let's take a closer look at why budgeting is so essential:

1. Financial Control:
   - A budget is a control tool that allows tracking every euro coming in and going out. This level of detail provides a clear view of expenses, helping identify areas where unnecessary spending can be cut, and focusing on what truly matters.

2. Planning and Financial Goals:
   - Budgeting is fundamental for short and long-term financial planning. It enables the establishment of realistic financial goals and the development of a strategy to achieve them. Whether saving for a home purchase or planning for retirement, a budget provides the necessary framework.

3. Prevention of Excessive Debt:

- Well-managed budget acts as a barrier against excessive debt. Monitoring expenses helps keep finances in check and avoids living beyond one's means, thereby reducing the risk of uncontrolled indebtedness.

4. Financial Sustainability:

- Budgeting promotes financial sustainability. Being aware of one's finances and striking a balance between income and expenses contributes to building a solid financial foundation, enabling coping with daily expenses and planning for the future.

5. Saving and Investments:

- Through budgeting, it's possible to identify saving and investment opportunities. Allocating a portion of income to savings and investments is crucial for wealth growth over time.

6. Adaptability to Changes:

- Life is dynamic, and budgeting offers the flexibility needed to adapt to changes in financial circumstances. A well-structured budget can be adjusted to address new expenses, income variations, or financial emergencies.

7. Reduction of Financial Stress:

- Financial awareness resulting from budgeting contributes to reducing financial stress. Knowing exactly where every euro goes provides a sense of control, reducing anxiety related to financial matters.

"A budget tells your financial story. Count every euro and make every euro count." - Tsh Oxenreider

In summary, budgeting is a powerful tool that goes beyond simply counting expenses. It is a means to achieve financial goals, reduce the risk of indebtedness, and create a solid financial future.

How to Identify and Categorize Expenses

Accurately identifying and categorizing expenses are crucial steps in creating an effective budget. This process allows for a clear overview of spending habits and provides the foundation for mindful financial management. Let's explore how to identify and categorize expenses effectively:

1. Record All Transactions:
   - The first step is to record all financial transactions. Use bank statements, receipts, and online information to gather accurate data on expenses. Finance management apps or software can simplify this process.

2. Divide Expenses into Categories:
   - Organize expenses into clear and understandable categories. For example, you might have categories such as Housing, Food, Transportation, Entertainment, Health and Wellness, Savings, etc. This breakdown offers a detailed view of various spending areas.

3. Fixed and Variable Expenses:
   - Differentiate between fixed and variable expenses. Fixed expenses are constant and regular, such as rent or mortgage, utilities, and subscriptions. Variable expenses may include food, leisure, and other non-regular purchases.

4. Analyze Spending Patterns:
   - Examine your data to identify spending patterns. This could reveal consumption habits or areas where improvements can be made. For instance, you might discover that you spend more than expected on restaurants or impulse purchases.

5. Spending Priorities:

- Prioritize spending categories based on your needs and financial goals. This can help you determine where to focus most of your resources and where expenses can be reduced.

6. Monitor Variable Expenses:

- Variable expenses, like entertainment or non-essential purchases, are often areas where cuts can be made without compromising basic needs. Monitor these categories closely to avoid surprises in spending.

7. Use Financial Management Tools:

- Utilize financial management tools, such as apps or software, that can automate expense categorization. These tools simplify the process of monitoring and analyzing spending habits.

8. Periodic Review:

- Don't forget to periodically review your expense categories. Life is dynamic, and your financial priorities may change over time. Regular analysis helps ensure that the budget adapts to your evolving needs.

"The control of expenses is the first rule of prosperity." - Thomas Jefferson

Accurately identifying and categorizing expenses is a fundamental step in creating an effective budget. In the next chapter, we will explore how to use this information to create and manage a realistic and sustainable budget.

Practical Tools for Budget Creation

Creating an effective budget requires the use of practical tools that simplify the process and provide a clear view of personal finances. Here are some practical tools that can be used to facilitate the creation and management of a budget:

1. Spreadsheets (Excel, Google Sheets):
   - Spreadsheets are a flexible and customizable tool for budget creation. You can use predefined templates or create your own spreadsheet. Formulas and functions can be employed to automate calculations and monitor income and expenses over time.

2. Financial Management Apps:
   - There are numerous financial management apps designed to streamline the budget creation process. Some of these apps

directly connect to your bank accounts, automatically categorize transactions, and offer clear visualizations of your finances.

3. Online Budgeting Software:

- Some dedicated budgeting software offers advanced features. They allow syncing bank accounts, generating detailed reports, setting financial goals, and monitoring spending trends.

4. Envelope Budgeting:

- This approach involves allocating a specific amount of money into physical or virtual envelopes for different expense categories (food, entertainment, etc.). When an envelope is empty, spending for that category is limited until the next month.

5. Online Financial Planners:

- Some websites provide financial planning tools that include budget creation. These tools guide the user through the process of identifying expenses and help establish realistic financial goals.

6. Financial Counseling Services:

- Financial counseling services offer professional assistance in creating a personalized budget. A financial counselor can assess your specific situation, provide customized advice, and help establish long-term financial plans.

7. Personal Financial Planners:

- Personal financial planners, both physical and virtual, can offer support in creating and managing a budget. These professionals have specific expertise in personal finance management and can provide tailored advice.

8. Online Budget Calculators:

- Websites offering online budget calculators allow users to input their income and expenses to get an instant snapshot of their financial situation. These tools are often free and easy to use.

Using practical tools for budget creation is crucial to maintaining financial control. In the next chapter, we will explore how to successfully implement and manage a personalized budget, ensuring it serves as a useful tool in guiding daily financial decisions.

CHAPTER 3

Smart Saving and Investing

Implementing and managing a personalized budget requires discipline, awareness, and flexibility. In this chapter, we will explore practical steps to make your budget an effective guide in the day-to-day management of finances.

The concept of personal budgeting has ancient roots. In ancient Rome, families kept detailed records of their income and expenses, carefully planning to ensure financial security. This practice has endured over time, adapting to the changing dynamics of modern society.

Steps to Implement an Effective Budget:

1. Clearly Define Expense Categories:
   - Based on the expense analysis from the previous chapter, clearly define the expense categories in your budget. Ensure they are specific and relevant to your financial situation.

2. Set Spending Limits for Each Category:
   - Assign a spending limit to each category. This limit should be realistic and reflect your financial priorities. For example, if saving for a trip is a priority, allocate a significant portion to the "Travel" category.

3. Monitor Expenses Regularly:

- Monitor your expenses regularly, preferably weekly or monthly. Use budgeting tools or apps to track transactions and ensure compliance with spending limits.

4. Flexibility and Adaptation:

- Life is dynamic, and your budget should be flexible. If unexpected expenses arise or your priorities change, adjust the budget accordingly. Adaptability is crucial for the long-term sustainability of your financial plan.

5. Automatic Savings:

- Automate savings through automatic transfers to a dedicated account. This will help you achieve your savings goals without having to manually transfer funds each time.

6. Plan for Future Expenses:

- Anticipate future expenses and plan accordingly. For instance, if you know you'll have annual expenses like car taxes, create a monthly plan to cover these costs.

7. Involve Your Partner or Family:

- If you have a partner or family, involve them in the creation and management of the budget. Collaboration increases a sense of responsibility and ensures everyone is aligned with common financial goals.

Practical Examples:

Let's say your budget includes an "Entertainment" category with a monthly limit of 150 euros. If halfway through the month you've already spent 120 euros, you can decide to reduce spending for the rest of the month or reallocate funds from a less prioritized category.

"A budget is a way of loving yourself." - Carrie Smith Nicholson

Successfully implementing and managing a personalized budget requires commitment and awareness.

Strategies for Saving
Money Every Day

Daily savings play a crucial role in maintaining a healthy budget and achieving financial goals. Here are some practical strategies to save money every day:

1. Meal Planning in Advance:
   - Prepare a weekly meal plan, create a shopping list, and only buy what you need. This reduces impulse purchases and minimizes food waste.

2. Seek Deals and Discounts:
   - Use apps or websites that offer discounts and deals on products and services. Before making purchases, look for online coupons or take advantage of promotions to save money.

3. Cut Back on Coffee Expenses:

- Limit buying coffee outside. Invest in a quality coffee maker and brew coffee at home. Even small daily savings can add up over time.

4. Save on Energy:
   - Turn off lights and appliances when not in use. Use energy-efficient LED bulbs. These actions can help reduce energy bills.

5. Avoid Impulse Purchases:
   - Set a reflection period before making unplanned purchases. Ask yourself if the purchase is truly necessary and if it fits within your budget.

6. Buy Discounted or Used Products:
   - Look for discounted or second-hand products. Often, you can find high-quality items at more affordable prices than new ones.

7. Use Public or Shared Transportation:
   - If possible, use public transportation or consider car-sharing. This can reduce the costs associated with owning and maintaining a car.

8. Trim Clothing Expenses:
   - Purchase clothing during sales or special offers. Reduce impulse buys of clothes that may not be essential.

9. Plan Outings in Advance:
   - Plan recreational outings in advance. This allows you to search for deals on events or activities and avoid excessive spending.

10. Limit Online Entertainment Expenses:
   - Evaluate your spending on online subscriptions. Cut down on the number of streaming services or other subscriptions you don't use frequently.

11. Change Eating Habits:

- Cook at home more often and eat out less frequently. This is not only healthier but can also significantly contribute to savings.

12. Negotiate Fees and Charges:

- Review your periodic bills, such as phone, internet, or insurance bills. If possible, try to negotiate more favorable rates.

"Saving is not necessarily determined by how much you earn but by how much you can retain." - Benjamin Franklin

Integrating these strategies into your daily life can significantly contribute to maintaining a balanced budget.

Introduction to the World
of Investments

Investing is a fundamental step for wealth growth and achieving long-term financial goals. This chapter introduces the world of investments, examining fundamental concepts and available opportunities.

Investing has a long history dating back to ancient times. In ancient Rome, citizens could participate in "collective investment societies" to fund projects. Over the centuries, the world of investments has evolved, integrating a wide range of tools and opportunities.

Fundamental Concepts of Investments:

1. Return and Risk:
   - Investing always involves a trade-off between return and risk. Investing in higher-return assets often implies a higher level of risk. Balancing these variables is important based on your financial goals and risk tolerance.

2. Diversification:
   - Diversifying the portfolio means investing in a variety of assets to reduce overall risk. Proper diversification can help mitigate losses in case of underperformance in a specific investment.

3. Financial Goals:
   - Investments should align with your financial goals. Whether saving for retirement, children's education, or a major purchase, the choice of investments will depend on the objectives you aim to achieve.

4. Time Horizon:
   - Time horizon is crucial in investments. Short-term investments might be more suitable for immediate goals, while long-term investments, such as retirement, can tolerate higher market fluctuations.

Investment Opportunities:

1. Stocks and Bonds:

- Stocks and bonds are among the most common tools. Stocks represent ownership in a company, while bonds are debt securities issued by entities like governments or corporations.

2. Mutual Funds:

- Mutual funds pool money from various investors to buy a diverse range of assets. They are professionally managed and offer diversification even to investors with limited capital.

3. Exchange-Traded Funds (ETFs):

- ETFs are similar to mutual funds but traded on stock exchanges like stocks. They provide diversification and are often more liquid.

4. Real Estate Investments:

- Real estate investments involve purchasing properties for income generation or appreciation over time. They can include houses, apartments, or investments in real estate funds.

5. Retirement Plans and 401(k):

- Corporate pension plans and individual plans like 401(k) provide structured ways to invest for retirement, often with tax advantages.

"Don't wait to invest, invest and wait." - Robert Kiyosaki

Investing is a key component of long-term wealth building. In the next chapter, we will explore how to integrate investments into your personal financial plan, considering risk management strategies and methods to monitor your portfolio's performance.

How to Start Investing Even with Small Sums

Investing is no longer reserved solely for those with substantial capital. Even with relatively small amounts, you can embark on an investment journey that may lead to significant growth over time. Here are some steps to begin investing with small sums:

1. Set Clear Goals:
   - Before diving into investing, clearly define your financial objectives. Whether you are saving for a vacation, a home purchase, or retirement, having clear goals will guide your investment decisions.

2. Create a Budget:
   - Understanding your income and expenses is crucial. A well-structured budget will help you determine how much you can allocate to investments without compromising your daily needs.

3. Eliminate High-Interest Debt:
   - Consider addressing high-interest debt before starting to invest. Reducing the burden of debt frees up more funds for investments and lowers overall financial risk.

4. Start with Mutual Funds:

- Mutual funds are an excellent starting point. They allow you to invest in a diverse range of assets even with small sums. Regular contributions can be automated.

5. Explore ETFs:

- Exchange-Traded Funds (ETFs) are similar to mutual funds but traded on the stock exchange. They are often more cost-effective and offer greater flexibility. You can even buy a single share.

6. Plan Your Purchases:

- Employ the "dollar-cost averaging" technique, investing a fixed amount regularly, regardless of market movements. This can mitigate the long-term impact of market volatility.

7. Utilize Micro-Investment Apps:

- Micro-investment apps like Acorns or Stash allow you to invest small sums by rounding up your daily expenses. This makes investing a continuous and less burdensome process.

8. Participate in Employer Retirement Plans:

- If your employer offers a company retirement plan, participate. Many of these programs allow automatic contributions directly from your salary.

9. Open an Automatic Savings Account:

- Some banks offer automatic savings accounts that automatically invest a portion of your savings in financial instruments. This is an effortless way to start investing.

10. Financial Education:

- Invest time in financial education. Understanding basic investment principles will make you more confident in your decisions and enable you to optimize your choices.

"Start investing. The goal is to make money work for you, not to work for money." - Idowu Koyenikan

Beginning to invest with small sums requires discipline and a well-thought-out strategy.

CHAPTER 4

Debt Management

The chapter on debt management is a crucial piece in constructing a solid financial foundation. Let's delve into the importance of understanding, monitoring, and reducing debt, incorporating current examples and wise reflections from financial experts.

In the words of Dave Ramsey, "Debt is like any other trap, easy to get into, but hard to get out of." We reflect on the stories of those who have learned to navigate the turbulent waters of debt.

1. Definition and Types of Debt:

   - Practical Example: Start by understanding debt. Differentiate between good and bad debt, identify the types of debt influencing your financial life, such as mortgages, student loans, and credit cards.

   - Reflection: "Debt isn't always negative. The key is understanding which debt serves your goals and which is an obstacle to your financial well-being." - Suze Orman

2. Debt Monitoring:

   - Practical Example: Keep track of your debt. Creating a comprehensive inventory, including balances, interest rates, and due dates, will provide a clear overview of your financial situation.

- "Knowing your debt is the first step to freeing yourself from it. Constant monitoring is the key to staying in control." - Dave Ramsey

3. Creating a Repayment Plan:

- Develop a repayment plan. Prioritize high-interest debts and work on a repayment plan that fits your financial resources.

- A repayment plan is your map to debt freedom. Be disciplined and stick to the plan with determination.

4. Techniques to Reduce Debt:

- Explore techniques to reduce debt. From the "snowball" method to debt consolidation, choose the strategy that best fits your financial situation.

- "There are different paths to debt freedom. Choose the one that resonates with your goals and values." - Dave Ramsey

5. Financial Discipline:

- Financial discipline is key. Resisting the temptation to accumulate new debt requires discipline. Set clear goals and stay focused on your repayment plan.

- "Discipline is the glue that holds your repayment plan together. Cultivate it as a fundamental skill." - Suze Orman

6. Creating a Support Network:

- Involve friends or family in your fight against debt. Creating a support network can provide motivation and encouragement when you need it most.

- Debt management can be a challenging journey. A support network offers the necessary support to face challenges with confidence.

7. Impact of Debt on Financial Health:

   - Understand the impact of debt on your overall financial health. Reducing debt frees up financial resources for investments and wealth building.

   - Debt can be an obstacle to your prosperity.

Understanding and Reducing Debt

Debt can be a significant burden on personal finances, but comprehending how to manage and reduce it is crucial for building a solid financial foundation.

Financial history is replete with examples of how debt can influence people's lives. From ancient Italian bankers in the Renaissance offering high-interest loans to modern financial crises, debt has played a significant role in economic history.

Understanding Debt:

1. Types of Debt:
   - Before tackling debt, it's essential to understand the different types. Debt can be classified into good debt (such as a mortgage for a home) and bad debt (e.g., high-interest loans).

2. Assessing the Importance of Debt:
   - Not all debt is equal. A low-interest mortgage for a home purchase may represent a long-term investment, while debt accumulated through impulsive purchases can be detrimental to

finances.

3. Comparing Interest Rates:

- Understanding interest rates is crucial. Reducing debt with higher interest rates should be a priority, as they significantly increase the total amount to be repaid over time.

Effectively Managing Debt:

1. Create a Repayment Plan:

- Establish a structured repayment plan. List all debts, organized from the highest to the lowest interest, and plan how to gradually repay them.

2. Negotiate with Creditors:

- Don't hesitate to negotiate with creditors. Many creditors may be willing to lower interest rates or offer more favorable payment plans if you communicate your difficulties.

3. Repayment Prioritization:

- Focus on repayment priorities. For example, debts with high-interest rates should be addressed first, while debts with lower rates can be tackled gradually.

4. Avoid New Debts:

- Stop accumulating new debts. Work on managing your finances so that you can live within your means and save instead of accruing further debt.

Strategies for Debt Reduction:

1. Debt Consolidation:

- Explore the option of debt consolidation, involving obtaining a new loan to pay off existing debts. This can simplify payments and reduce interest rates.

2. Selling Non-Essential Assets:

- If possible, consider selling non-essential assets to generate extra funds to reduce debt. It can be a quick way to address financial obligations.

3. Increase Income:

- Explore opportunities to increase income, such as seeking part-time work or developing skills that can lead to extra earnings.

"Take care of debt so that it doesn't grow into a chronic financial ailment." - Suze Orman

Dealing with debt requires discipline and a well-defined strategy.

Strategies for Debt Consolidation

Debt consolidation is a strategy that can simplify financial management, reduce interest rates, and make payments more manageable. In this chapter, we will explore strategies for consolidating debts and reducing the overall financial burden.

Throughout history, the need to streamline debts and reduce financial burdens has always been present. Even in ancient Rome, debt consolidation mechanisms were employed to facilitate repayment.

Strategies for Debt Consolidation:

1. Debt Consolidation Loans:
   - One of the most common approaches is obtaining a debt consolidation loan. This loan is used to pay off all existing debts, creating a single monthly payment with often more favorable interest rates.

2. Zero-Interest Balance Transfer Credit Cards:
   - Some credit cards offer zero-interest balance transfer promotions. You can transfer balances from existing credit cards to a new card, benefiting from an interest-free period to pay off the debt.

3. Asset-Backed Secured Loans:
   - If you own valuable assets, such as your home, you may consider a secured loan. This involves using the asset as collateral to secure a loan with lower interest rates.

4. Negotiate with Creditors:
   - Do not hesitate to negotiate with your current creditors. Often, they may be willing to reduce interest rates or offer more favorable repayment plans, especially if you communicate financial difficulties.

5. *Credit Counseling:
   - Seeking advice from a credit counselor can be helpful. Non-profit organizations offer counseling services that can assist you in creating a personalized debt consolidation plan.

Phases of the Debt Consolidation Process:

1. Financial Situation Assessment:
   - Before consolidating debts, carefully assess your financial situation. Understand the total debts, interest rates, and your available budget.

2. Choosing the Consolidation Option:

- Select the consolidation option that best suits your needs. The choice will depend on your financial situation, available interest rates, and your ability to provide collateral.

3. Application and Approval:

- Submit your application for the debt consolidation loan or zero-interest balance transfer credit card. Ensure you understand the terms and conditions before proceeding.

4. Settling Existing Debts:

- Once you've obtained the loan or transferred balances, use the funds to pay off all existing debts. This streamlines payments, consolidating them into a single monthly installment.

5. Continuous Monitoring:

- After consolidation, consistently monitor your financial situation. Ensure you adhere to the new terms and try to avoid accumulating new debts.

Consolidating debts requires a thorough understanding of one's financial situation and available options. In the next chapter, we will further explore the path to sound financial management.

Preventing Excessive Debt Accumulation

Preventing the excessive accumulation of debt is a key strategy for maintaining long-term financial health. In this chapter, we will explore proactive approaches to avoid excessive debt accumulation and promote responsible financial management.

Throughout financial history, excessive debt accumulation has been a recurring issue. From sovereign debt crises to the 2008 financial crisis, historical episodes teach us the importance of preventing and responsibly managing debt.

Strategies to Prevent Excessive Debt Accumulation:

1. Create a Realistic Budget:
   - A realistic budget is essential for understanding your income, expenses, and setting clear limits. Monitor your finances closely to avoid excessive spending.

2. Save Before Purchasing:
   - Before making significant purchases, save a portion of the necessary money. This will reduce the need to resort to debt to meet your needs.

3. Avoid Impulse Purchases:
   - Resisting impulse purchases is crucial. Take the necessary time to reflect on unplanned purchases, thus avoiding regret and unnecessary debt accumulation.

4. Establish Financial Priorities:
   - Identify your financial priorities and focus your resources on them. This could include repaying existing debt or saving for long-term financial goals.

5. Responsible Use of Credit Cards:

- Use credit cards responsibly. Pay the full balance each month to avoid high-interest charges. Also, limit the number of credit cards to reduce the temptation of accumulating too much debt.

6. Create an Emergency Fund:

- An emergency fund can help you handle unforeseen expenses without resorting to debt. Save regularly to build a financial safety net.

7. Plan for Major Purchases:

- For significant purchases, such as a home or a car, plan carefully. Save for the down payment and explore financing options with competitive interest rates.

8. Avoid High-Risk Loans:

- Steer clear of high-risk loans with high-interest rates. Always seek more favorable financing options or consider waiting and saving before making certain purchases.

Personal and Financial Growth:

1. Invest in Financial Education:

- Investing time and energy in financial education can help you make more informed decisions, reducing the risk of harmful financial choices.

2. Income Growth:

- Look for opportunities to increase your income. Income growth can provide greater financial flexibility and reduce dependence on debt.

"Preventing debt is an act of financial self-care." - Suze Orman

Preventing excessive debt accumulation requires financial discipline and awareness of spending habits. In the next chapter, we will further explore strategies for planning the future, focusing on long-term financial planning.

CHAPTER 5

Building an Emergency Fund

The chapter on building an emergency fund is a crucial step in ensuring short-term financial stability. In this chapter, we explore the importance of an emergency fund, how much it should be, and practical strategies for creating it.

Let's reflect on the wisdom of Franklin D. Roosevelt, who said, "Be prepared. Wisdom is the fruit of prudence, not fear."

1. Importance and Purpose of the Emergency Fund:

- Understand the importance and purpose of the emergency fund. This fund is designed to cover unexpected expenses such as medical care, home repairs, or loss of income.

- The emergency fund is your financial lifesaver. It's not an expense but an investment in your financial security.

2. How Much Should Your Emergency Fund Be:

- Determine the size of your emergency fund. Many experts recommend having at least three to six months' worth of monthly expenses as a reserve to handle critical situations.

- "The exact amount may vary, but the larger your emergency fund, the greater your peace of mind." - Dave Ramsey

3. Strategies for Building and Maintaining the Emergency Fund:

- Implement practical strategies. Save a portion of your income every month, automate transfers to a separate account, and resist the temptation to use the fund for non-urgent expenses.

- Building an emergency fund requires consistency and discipline. Every small contribution is a step toward your financial security.

4. Use the Fund Only for Emergencies:

- Respect the purpose of the fund. Use the emergency fund only for unexpected and critical expenses, avoiding withdrawals for unnecessary purchases.

- The temptation to use the fund for short-term desires is real, but your financial security depends on your discipline.

5. Regularly Update the Emergency Fund:

- Regularly update your emergency fund. Review your expenses and adjust the fund to meet your evolving needs.

- "Life changes, and your emergency fund should adapt to these changes. Periodic reviews keep the fund effective." - Suze Orman

6. Options for Investing the Emergency Fund:

- Explore safe options for investing your emergency fund. Certificates of deposit (CDs) or money market accounts may offer better returns than traditional savings accounts.

- "Safety is a priority, but seeking options that at least cover inflation is a wise step." - Dave Ramsey

7. Job Loss Emergency Reserve:

- Maintain a specific emergency reserve for job loss. This should cover essential expenses during the period of seeking new employment.

- "Job loss is one of the most critical times. Having a dedicated

reserve can alleviate the financial burden during those moments."
- Suze Orman

8. Handle Emergencies Without Using the Fund:

- Develop the ability to handle emergencies without tapping into the emergency fund. Adequate insurance and prudent expense management can reduce the need to use the fund frequently.

- Preventing emergencies is as important as being prepared to face them. Risk management is a crucial part of your financial strategy.

Conclusions:

Building an emergency fund is like constructing a bulwark against financial uncertainty. One step at a time, with consistency and determination, you can build a reserve that provides you with security and financial flexibility. Whether you're starting your fund or strengthening it, remember that your peace of mind is a valuable investment. Embark on this journey with wisdom because a robust emergency fund is your ally in navigating financial storms.

Importance and Purpose of
the Emergency Fund

The emergency fund is a fundamental element in personal financial management. In this chapter, we will explore the importance and purpose of an emergency fund, providing practical advice on how to create and manage one effectively.

While the concept of an emergency fund doesn't have a specific history, human societies have always faced unforeseen events and crises. However, the formalization of an emergency fund has become more widespread with the evolution of personal financial practices.

Importance of the Emergency Fund:

1. Dealing with Unforeseen Expenses:
   - An emergency fund provides a financial safety net to deal with unforeseen expenses such as medical care, home or vehicle repairs, or loss of employment.

2. Reducing Dependence on Debt:
   - When emergencies occur, the temptation to resort to debt is high. An emergency fund reduces dependence on credit, safeguarding your long-term financial situation.

3. Planning for Transition Periods:
   - Transition periods, such as moving from one job to another or experiencing unemployment, can be more manageable with an emergency fund covering basic expenses.

4. Ensuring Psychological Security:
   - Knowing you have an emergency fund provides psychological security. This reduces financial stress, allowing you to focus

on solutions rather than worrying about immediate financial difficulties.

Purpose of the Emergency Fund:

1. Covering Essential Expenses:
   - The primary purpose of an emergency fund is to cover essential expenses such as rent, bills, food, and medical care during a crisis.

2. Avoiding High-Interest Debt:
   - An emergency fund enables you to avoid resorting to high-interest debts, such as credit cards or personal loans, in emergency situations.

3. Ensuring Financial Continuity: - It ensures financial continuity during exceptional situations, such as a pandemic, natural disaster, or global economic crises, by providing a solid financial foundation.

4. Planning for the Future:
   - Regularly contributing to an emergency fund is part of long-term financial planning. It ensures you are prepared to face future challenges.

Effective Management of the Emergency Fund:

1. Establishing a Savings Goal:
   - Set a realistic savings goal for your emergency fund. Experts recommend aiming for at least three to six months of essential expenses.

2. Regular Contributions:
   - Contribute regularly to your emergency fund. You can set up automatic transfers to ensure the fund grows consistently.

3. Periodic Reviews:
   - Periodically review your emergency fund to ensure it is

adequate based on your current financial needs and changes in your life.

4. Avoiding Unnecessary Use:

- Use the fund only for genuine emergencies. Resisting the temptation to use it for non-essential expenses contributes to its long-term effectiveness.

"The emergency fund is like a parachute - better to have it and not need it than need it and not have it." - Anonymous

An emergency fund is the pillar of financial stability and can make a difference during challenging times.

How Much Should Your Emergency Fund Be

The size of your emergency fund is crucial, as it should be robust enough to handle unexpected expenses without creating an undue financial burden. In this chapter, we will explore how to determine the appropriate size of your emergency fund and provide practical guidelines to achieve this goal.

1. Calculate Essential Expenses:

- Start by calculating your monthly essential expenses. These include rent or mortgage, bills, food, medical care, and other necessary costs. Multiply this figure by the number of months you wish to cover with your emergency fund.

2. Consider Job Stability:

- Evaluate the stability of your job and the industry you work in. If you work in an unstable sector or on short-term contracts, it might be wise to have a larger emergency fund.

3. Contemplate Personal Circumstances:

- Consider your personal circumstances. For instance, if you have a family or depend on a single income, a larger emergency fund may be necessary to cover the needs of all family members.

4. Aim for Three to Six Months of Expenses:

- A common goal for an emergency fund is to cover at least three to six months of essential expenses. This should provide you with a sufficient safety net during periods of crisis or financial instability.

5. Account for Liabilities:

- Consider liabilities, such as ongoing debts and loans. An emergency fund should also be able to cover the monthly payments of such obligations to avoid resorting to debt in emergency situations.

6. Factor in Risks and Unexpected Expenses:

- Plan for risks and unexpected expenses. For example, you may need to deal with unforeseen medical costs or significant repairs in your home or vehicle.

7. Update Periodically:

- Periodically update the size of your emergency fund. Events like changes in employment status or family economic circumstances may require a reassessment of the required amount.

"Planning the size of your emergency fund is a form of financial self-defense, a demonstration of responsibility toward your future." - Suze Orman

Determining the appropriate size of your emergency fund requires a thoughtful assessment of your needs and circumstances.

Strategies for Building and Maintaining an Emergency Fund

The effective construction and management of an emergency fund are crucial for ensuring long-term financial security. In this chapter, we will explore practical strategies to build your emergency fund and maintain it effectively over time.

1. Set Monthly Savings Goals:
   - Establish realistic and achievable monthly savings goals. Creating a plan helps you stay in control of your finances and ensures that you are consistently building your emergency fund.

2. Automate Transfers:
   - Automate monthly transfers to your emergency fund. Set up an automatic transfer from your checking account to the emergency fund account to ensure that the savings process happens effortlessly.

3. Trim Non-Essential Expenses:
   - Scrutinize your expenses closely and look for opportunities to cut non-essential ones. The money saved can be directed towards your emergency fund.

4. Use Extra Income:
   - Use extra income to fuel your emergency fund. Bonuses, gifts, or occasional windfalls can present an opportunity to make a significant contribution.

5. Seek Additional Income:
   - Consider the opportunity to earn additional income through part-time jobs, freelance work, or side activities. This extra

income stream can be directed straight to the emergency fund.

6. Sell Unnecessary Items:

- If you have unnecessary belongings, consider selling them to generate additional funds for your emergency fund. This could include household items, clothing, or equipment you no longer use.

7. Receive a Pay Raise? Increase Savings:

- If you receive a salary increase or promotion, seize the opportunity to raise your monthly contribution to the emergency fund rather than increasing lifestyle expenses.

8. Use Tax Refunds:

- If you receive a tax refund, consider allocating a portion or the entire amount to your emergency fund. This can help rapidly grow your financial safety net.

9. Avoid Using the Fund for Non-Emergencies:

- Reserve your emergency fund solely for genuine emergency situations. Avoid using it for non-emergencies to ensure its steady growth.

10. Periodically Reassess Your Goal:

- Periodically reassess the target amount for your emergency fund. Changes in your life or financial circumstances may require an adjustment to the desired amount.

"Building an emergency fund is like constructing a financial fortress, one stone at a time." - Dave Ramsey

The deliberate construction and management of your emergency fund are fundamental to ensuring lasting financial stability. In the next chapter, we will explore retirement planning and the importance of safeguarding against unforeseen events.

CHAPTER 6

Retirement Planning and Insurance

In the sixth chapter, we will address two crucial aspects of long-term financial security: retirement planning and the importance of safeguarding against unforeseen events. We will explore strategies to ensure a stable financial future and protect against unexpected risks.

Let's reflect on the wisdom of John C. Bogle, founder of Vanguard, who said, "Long-term investment is your best friend when it comes to retirement planning."

"Pension is a life phase to be carefully planned. It's your gift to your future self, so invest wisely." - Suze Orman

1. The Importance of Retirement Planning:

   - Understand the importance of retirement planning. Retirement marks a chapter in life where income no longer comes from active work; therefore, plan carefully to maintain a comfortable lifestyle.

2. Types of Insurance to Consider:

   - Explore various types of insurance. Life, health, auto, and disability insurance are just a few options to consider for protecting yourself and your family.

3. Balancing Insurance Coverage and Retirement Savings:

- Find the balance between insurance coverage and retirement savings. Excessive coverage can strain your budget, but insufficient insurance might leave you vulnerable.

- "The key is finding balance. Ensure you have necessary coverage without compromising your retirement savings efforts." - Suze Orman

4. Individual and Employer Retirement Planning:

- Examine individual and employer retirement planning options. From 401(k) plans to IRAs, understand which tools are available and best suit your needs.

5. Investment Diversification in Retirement Planning:

- Diversify investments in your retirement planning. A well-balanced portfolio reduces risk and enhances long-term return opportunities.

- "Diversification is the key to success in retirement planning. Don't put all your eggs in one basket." - Suze Orman

6. Retirement Planning for Different Life Stages:

- Tailor your retirement planning to different life stages. Priorities and needs change, so update your retirement plan accordingly.

7. Using Tax Tools in Retirement Planning:

- Leverage available tax tools. Tax-deductible contributions, such as those to a 401(k) or a traditional IRA, can offer significant tax benefits.

- "Smart retirement planning goes hand in hand with efficient tax management. Take advantage of available tax incentives."

8. Retirement Planning for a Lasting Legacy:

- Consider retirement planning for a lasting legacy. Structure your plan to be seamlessly transferable, ensuring a secure financial future for your loved ones.

9. Family Protection Insurances:

- Invest in insurances that protect your family. A life insurance policy can ensure your loved ones are financially secure in your absence.

- "Life insurance is an act of love for your family. It provides security and peace of mind in challenging times." - Suze Orman

Conclusions:

Retirement planning and risk management through insurance are two fundamental pillars of financial stability. Prepare for the future with careful planning and protect yourself and your family from the unexpected. Approach retirement with wisdom and build a safety net that accompanies you through life's stages. With thoughtful planning, you'll be able to enjoy a fulfilling retirement and face life with the peace of mind that comes from financial security.

The Importance of Retirement Planning

Retirement planning is a crucial element in ensuring financial security during the retirement years. In this chapter, we will explore the importance of initiating retirement planning early, providing practical advice on preparing for a stable financial future.

Throughout history, people often worked until physically unable, lacking a structured retirement plan. However, with changing work patterns and increased life expectancy, retirement has become a fundamental aspect of financial planning.

Importance of Retirement Planning:

1. Ensuring a Comfortable Life in Retirement:
   - Retirement is the phase of life where active work for earning a living cease. Thoughtful retirement planning ensures sufficient income to maintain a comfortable lifestyle even in advanced age.

2. Addressing Inflation:
   - Retirement planning considers inflation, ensuring that your pension income maintains its purchasing power over time. This is essential to prevent rising costs from eroding the value of your

money.

3. Supporting Medical Expenses:

- As age advances, medical expenses tend to increase. Proper retirement planning includes forecasting adequate funds to address medical expenses without compromising the quality of life.

4. Avoiding Dependency on Family:

- Sound retirement planning reduces the likelihood of financial dependence on family members or government assistance services. Maintaining financial independence is a key goal.

5. Creating an Estate Plan:

- Retirement planning may involve creating an estate plan to ensure heirs are adequately provided for. This could include asset management, life insurance, or establishing a trust.

6. Utilizing Tax Opportunities:

- In many jurisdictions, there are tax advantages associated with retirement. Thoughtful planning can help you make the most of these opportunities, minimizing the tax impact on your retirement savings.

Practical Tips for Effective Retirement Planning:

1. Start Early:

- Commencing retirement savings as early as possible offers the advantage of time. Even small amounts invested long-term can grow significantly.

2. Leverage Employer Retirement Plans:

- Utilize retirement plans offered by your employer, such as 401(k) or company pension plans. Regular contributions to these programs can provide a solid retirement fund.

3. Diversify Investments:

- Diversifying investments is crucial to shield your retirement portfolio from market fluctuations. Consult a financial advisor for a balanced investment strategy.

4. Periodically Reassess:

- Periodically reassess your retirement plan based on changes in your life, market conditions, and financial needs.

5. Consider Longevity Insurance:

- Longevity insurance is an option that provides additional income if you surpass a specific age. This can be a useful element in a retirement strategy.

Retirement planning is an investment in your future that can determine the quality of your life in your later years.

Types of Insurance to Consider

Risk management is a fundamental aspect of financial planning. In this chapter, we will explore various types of insurance that you should consider to protect yourself, your family, and your assets from unforeseen financial events.

1. Life Insurance:
- Life insurance provides a benefit in the event of the insured's death. It can be a key element in ensuring the financial security of your family in your absence. It can be term (short-term) or permanent (long-term).

2. Health Insurance:
- Health insurance covers medical expenses, helping prevent unforeseen medical costs from becoming a financial burden. It may include coverage for doctor visits, medications, hospitalizations, and specialized care.

3. Disability Insurance:
- This type of insurance provides income in the event of a disability that prevents you from working. It can be crucial to maintaining income and addressing daily expenses if you become unable to work.

4. Auto Insurance:
- Auto insurance is mandatory in many jurisdictions and provides coverage for vehicle damage or injuries to individuals resulting from road accidents. It may also include coverage against theft and damage from natural events.

5. Home Insurance:
- Protects your residence from damages and losses, such as fires, floods, theft, or structural damage. Home insurance can also cover the contents of the house, offering comprehensive protection.

6. Liability Insurance:
- Liability insurance covers damages you may cause to third-party individuals or properties. It is essential to protect your assets in case of legal actions against you.

7. Income Insurance:
- Income insurance provides financial support in case of income loss due to illness or injury preventing you from working. It is particularly important for self-employed individuals or those

dependent on their income.

8. Accident Insurance:

- This insurance offers specific financial coverage in the event of accidental injuries leading to disability or injury. It can be a valuable addition, especially for those engaged in high-risk occupations.

9. Longevity Insurance:

- Longevity insurance provides additional income after reaching a certain age. This can be useful to ensure financial coverage during retirement years.

10. Travel Insurance:

- Travel insurance covers medical expenses, trip cancellations, loss of luggage, and other unforeseen events during travels. It is essential, especially for international trips.

11. Education Insurance:

- This type of insurance is designed to ensure the continuity of your children's education in case of your absence or disability. It may cover school or university expenses.

Choosing the right insurances depends on your individual needs and financial situation. Consulting with a industry professional can help you design a personalized insurance strategy.

Balancing Insurance Coverage and Retirement Savings

Balancing insurance coverage and retirement savings is a crucial challenge in financial planning. In this chapter, we will explore practical strategies to find the right balance between these two aspects, ensuring adequate protection while simultaneously building a robust retirement fund.

1. Evaluate Your Insurance Needs:
   - Start by assessing your insurance needs. Consider your family situation, health status, occupation, and financial responsibilities. This evaluation will help determine which types of insurance are essential for you.

2. Create an Adequate Coverage Plan:
   - Once needs are identified, create an adequate coverage plan. Ensure you have life insurance, health insurance, and other coverages that align with your specific requirements.

3. Avoid Over-Insurance:
   - Steers clear of over-insurance. It's not always necessary to have maximum coverage on every type of insurance. A realistic assessment of your needs can prevent excessive costs.

4. Consider Long-Term Insurance Options:
   - Some insurance policies, such as permanent life insurance, can also serve as a long-term investment. Carefully evaluate these options, balancing insurance coverage with value growth.

5. Strategically Plan Your Retirement:

- Build a solid retirement plan. Include regular contributions to employer pension programs, individual investments, and other retirement savings vehicles. The goal is to construct a retirement fund that can support your desired lifestyle post-retirement.

6. Diversify Pension Investments:

- Diversify investments in your retirement plan. This reduces risk and provides better long-term return opportunities. Consult a financial advisor to create a balanced portfolio.

7. Leverage Tax Benefits:

- Take advantage of tax benefits associated with pension contributions. Contributing to pension plans can reduce taxable income and offer significant tax savings.

8. Evaluate Combined Insurance Options:

- Some insurance policies offer combined options, such as life insurance with long-term care benefits. These solutions can provide multiple coverages in a single policy.

9. Periodically Reassess Your Plan:

- Your financial situation will change over time. Periodically reassess your insurance and retirement plan to ensure it aligns with changes in your life and financial goals.

10. Consider a Comprehensive Financial Plan:

- Think about a comprehensive financial plan. Look beyond insurance coverage and retirement savings, including debt management, investment, and tax planning.

Balancing insurance coverage and retirement savings requires thoughtful planning and ongoing assessment of your financial situation.

CHAPTER 7

Increasing Income

The seventh chapter will guide us through practical strategies to increase income and enhance financial well-being. We will explore ways to maximize current earnings and create opportunities for long-term income growth.

Let's reflect on the words of Jim Rohn, who said, "Work harder on yourself than you do on your job. If you work on your job, you'll make a living. If you work on yourself, you'll make a fortune."

1. Strategies to Improve Current Income:

   - Explore strategies to enhance your current income. This may include negotiating your salary, acquiring new skills to advance in your current career, or seeking growth opportunities within your current position.

2. Explore Additional Income Opportunities:

   - Explore additional income opportunities. Consider part-time jobs, freelance work, or side activities that can bring in an extra income stream.

   - Diversifying your income sources not only improves financial stability but also opens doors to new opportunities.

3. Develop Skills for Career Advancement:

- Develop skills that enhance your market value. Training courses, certifications, or degrees can make you more appealing to employers and open up more lucrative career opportunities.

- Your market value is directly proportional to the skills you possess. Invest in yourself to increase your value.

4. Leverage Freelance and Online Opportunities:

- Leverage freelance and online opportunities. The gig economy offers many earning possibilities, from virtual assistance to freelance writing.

- The online world provides a vast landscape for those seeking additional income opportunities. Use it wisely.

5. Create Passive Income Sources:

- Aim to create passive income sources. Invest in real estate, stocks that pay dividends, or start a blog or YouTube channel that can generate income over time.

6. Explore the World of Investments:

- Explore the world of investments. Investing wisely can lead to significant returns, contributing to increased income in the long run.

- "Investments are not just for financial experts. With a bit of knowledge and a well-thought-out strategy, anyone can make them work for themselves." - Dave Ramsey

7. Build Personal Brand and Network:

- Invest in your personal brand and building a strong network. A good reputation and meaningful connections can open doors to career opportunities and lucrative partnerships.

8. Seize Growth Opportunities in Current Job:

   - Seize growth opportunities within your current job. Look for promotions, special projects, or other chances that can lead to professional advancement and, consequently, income growth.

   - Working smart is as important as working hard. Seek opportunities that can grow your career.

9. Maintain a Work-Life Balance:

   - Maintain a balance between work and life. Your health and well-being are fundamental. Find ways to increase your income without sacrificing your quality of life.

   - Success is not only the result of your income but also of your overall happiness and well-being.

Conclusion:

Increasing income is not just a financial goal but a process of personal and professional growth. With a combination of skill improvement, seizing opportunities, and prudent income management, you can create a solid foundation for a prosperous financial future. Increasing income is not just a means to achieve your financial goals but also a journey toward personal and professional fulfillment.

Strategies to Improve Current Income

In this chapter, we will focus on practical strategies to enhance your current income. These strategies can contribute to ensuring greater financial stability in the present while also providing additional resources for future investments.

1. Upgrade Professional Skills:
   - Investing in improving your professional skills can increase your market attractiveness. Seek training courses or certifications relevant to your industry.

2. Explore Freelance or Part-Time Job Opportunities:
   - Consider working as a freelancer or part-time in fields related to your skills. This can be a way to earn extra money without committing to full-time employment.

3. Salary Negotiation:
   - If you believe your experience and skills warrant an increase, don't hesitate to negotiate your salary with your employer. Negotiation is common practice and can lead to a significant improvement in your income.

4. Explore Second Job Opportunities:
   - If circumstances allow, explore second job opportunities, perhaps in a sector aligned with your interests or skills. However, it's essential to balance additional work to avoid fatigue.

5. Create Passive Income:
   - Look for ways to create passive income. This can come from investments, real estate rentals, or even online activities such as blogging or selling digital products.

6. Sell Unnecessary Items:
   - Review your personal belongings and consider selling items you don't use or need. You can use online platforms to sell second-

hand items and earn extra income.

7. Enroll in Online Training Courses:

- Enroll in online training courses that can develop new skills and broaden your career opportunities. Many of these courses are accessible and offer significant value.

8. Create Online Content:

- If you have skills in a particular area, consider creating online content. This could include blogs, videos on platforms like YouTube, or participating in podcasts. Monetizing quality content can generate income.

9. Efficiently Manage Finances:

- Efficient financial management can free up resources. Review your budget, cut unnecessary expenses, and maximize savings. These funds can be reinvested or used to enhance your lifestyle.

10. Invest in High-Yield Opportunities:

- Explore investment opportunities that offer higher returns than traditional ones. This could include stocks, high-yield bonds, or real estate investments.

"Current income can be the launching pad for your future financial success. Invest in yourself today to reap the rewards tomorrow." - Anonymous

Improving your current income requires a mix of strategies, creativity, and commitment. In the next chapter, we will further explore the world of investments, focusing on how to begin investing even with small sums.

Exploring Additional Income Opportunities

In the context of a dynamic economy, exploring additional income opportunities can be an effective strategy to improve your financial situation. In this chapter, we will examine various avenues through which you can increase your earnings beyond your primary income.

1. Freelance and Part-Time Jobs:
   - Consider the opportunity to engage in freelance or part-time work in fields related to your skills. Many online platforms offer job opportunities for freelancers in areas such as writing, graphic design, programming, and more.

2. Real Estate Rentals:
   - If you own additional properties or have extra space in your home, renting can be an option to generate passive income. This could include renting a room, an apartment, or even your entire

home for short-term stays through vacation rental platforms.

3. Create Online Content:
- If you have skills or experiences in a particular field, creating online content can be an additional source of income. This may include blogging, producing videos on YouTube, or participating in podcasts.

4. Consulting or Coaching:
- If you are an expert in a specific field, offering consulting or coaching services can be a way to earn extra money. This could involve business consulting, life coaching, financial consulting, or other areas.

5. Freelance Consulting Work:
- Offer your services as a freelance consultant. Many companies seek external experts for specific projects, and this can be a great opportunity to utilize your skills and earn extra income.

6. Crafting and Selling Handmade Products:
- If you have artistic or craft skills, creating and selling handmade products can be an option. Online platforms like Etsy offer the opportunity to reach a wide audience.

7. Affiliate and Online Marketing:
- Explore affiliate programs or online marketing. Promoting other products or services and earning commissions on sales can be an effective way to generate additional income.

8. Temporary or Online Freelance Work:
- Take advantage of temporary or online freelance work opportunities. There are many platforms connecting workers with short-term projects, allowing you to earn based on your skills and availability.

9. Dividend Investments:
- Investing in stocks that pay regular dividends can provide a

source of passive income. Acquiring shares in stable companies with a history of dividends can create a steady income stream.

10. Create an Online Course:

- If you have in-depth knowledge of a specific topic, consider creating an online course. Platforms like Udemy or Teachable allow you to sell courses and earn income through online education.

Exploring additional income opportunities requires creativity, flexibility, and openness to new ideas.

Developing Skills to Advance
in Your Career

Now, let's explore the importance of skill development for advancing in your career. Investing in yourself is a crucial step to enhance professional opportunities and, consequently, increase your income.

1. Identify Key Skills:
   - Evaluate the industry you work in and identify the key skills required. This may include technical skills, leadership abilities, communication skills, or industry-specific expertise.

2. Training Courses and Certifications:
   - Take training courses and obtain certifications relevant to your field. This not only enhances your skills but also demonstrates to employers your commitment to improvement.

3. Master Classes and Workshops:
   - Attend master classes, workshops, and seminars conducted by industry experts. These events can provide insights and practical advice not easily obtained through traditional learning.

4. Mentorship and Networking:
   - Seek mentorship from experienced professionals in your field. Relationships with mentors can offer personalized guidance and valuable insights into your professional growth.

5. Online Training:
   - Utilize the wide range of online training resources. Platforms like LinkedIn Learning, Coursera, and edX offer courses on a variety of topics, allowing you to learn conveniently from your own home.

6. Participation in Industry Conferences:
   - Attend industry conferences and networking events. These gatherings not only keep you updated on the latest trends but also provide an opportunity to establish important connections in your field.

7. Soft Skills Development:

- Do not neglect the development of soft skills. Abilities such as effective communication, time management, and problem-solving are just as crucial as technical skills.

8. Involvement in Innovative Projects:

- Engage in innovative projects at your current workplace. Involvement in forward-thinking initiatives can make you stand out to leadership and create advancement opportunities.

9. Continuous Feedback:

- Seek continuous feedback on your performance. Understanding your strengths and areas for improvement can guide your development path.

10. Case Studies and Practical Applications:

- Apply what you have learned through case studies and practical applications. Practice is fundamental to solidify your skills and demonstrate your value in the field.

"The best investment you can make is in yourself. Personal growth is the key to unlocking new opportunities." - Jim Rohn

Skill development is a long-term investment that can open unexpected doors in your career.

CHAPTER 8

Tactics for Tax Savings

Chapter eight will take us into the complex yet crucial world of personal taxes. We will explore tactics and strategies to maximize net income through tax deductions and tax-saving plans.

Let's reflect on the wise words of Benjamin Franklin: "In this world, nothing can be said to be certain, except death and taxes."

Saving on taxes is an act of smart financial management. Every euro saved is a euro earned.

1. Understanding Personal Tax Laws:

   - Acquire knowledge about personal tax laws. Understanding tax regulations enables you to make the most of available deductions and tax incentives.

   - Tax laws change and adapt. Stay updated to maximize tax benefits.

2. Optimizing Tax Deductions:

   - Optimize tax deductions. From mortgage interest deductions to medical expenses, leverage all available deductions to reduce your tax burden.

   - Tax deductions are a legitimate way to decrease your tax liability. Don't leave money on the table.

3. Efficient Investments and Tax Plans:

- Plan efficient investments and tax strategies. Consider investments that offer tax advantages, such as tax-deductible retirement accounts or low-tax index funds.

- Efficient tax investments not only generate returns but also reduce your tax liability.

4. Utilizing Incentives for Retirement Planning:

- Utilize incentives for retirement planning. Contribute the maximum allowed to tax-deductible retirement plans to maximize tax benefits.

- Your retirement is not just for your future but also for your current tax situation. Take advantage of available incentives.

5. Using Tax Credits:

- Use tax credits. From child deductions to education credits, capitalize on opportunities to receive direct reductions in your tax liability.

6. Tax Planning for Additional Income:

- Plan your tax liability for additional income. If you earn from diverse sources, consider how to organize your activities to optimize taxation.

- Additional income is great, but thoughtful tax planning is what truly makes it profitable.

7. Deductions for Business Expenses:

- If you are an entrepreneur or freelancer, maximize deductions for business expenses. From your workspace to training costs, reduce taxable income through legitimate deductions.

- Your business can also be your tax ally. Know the rules and leverage available deductions.

8. Deepen Understanding of Local and State Taxes:

- Deepen your understanding of local and state taxes. Tax laws can vary, so understanding your local tax situation is essential to maximize tax benefits.

9. Collaborate with a Tax Professional:

- Collaborate with a tax professional. A tax expert can provide personalized advice to optimize your tax situation and ensure compliance with tax laws.

Conclusion:

Saving on taxes is a smart financial management tactic. With a thorough knowledge of personal tax laws and the implementation of savvy strategies, you can reduce your tax burden, freeing up resources to achieve your financial goals. However, it is essential to navigate this complex territory carefully. Your treasure map for tax savings is your knowledge, and your ideal travel companion is a reliable tax professional.

Understanding Personal Tax Laws

Comprehending the tax system is crucial to optimizing your financial situation, legally reducing the tax burden, and maximizing your available income.

Understanding Personal Tax Laws:

Knowledge of personal tax laws is a powerful tool for efficiently managing your finances. While the tax system may seem complex, a basic understanding allows you to leverage opportunities provided by tax deductions, benefits, and tax planning strategies.

Taxation is an ancient practice dating back to Ancient Greece and Rome. However, modern personal tax systems have roots in the 19th century when many Western countries adopted income taxes to fund the growing needs of the state.

Importance of Personal Tax Knowledge:

1. Maximizing Deductions:
   - Understanding tax deductions allows you to reduce taxable income. This may include deductions for education, medical expenses, home purchase loans, and more.

2. Optimizing Tax Regime:

- Choosing the most advantageous tax regime for your situation can make a significant difference. For example, you might benefit more from a joint or separate tax return, depending on your circumstances.

3. Tax Planning for Investments:

- Investing intelligently can minimize the tax impact. For instance, selling long-term assets may enjoy lower tax rates compared to short-term ones.

4. Utilizing Tax-Saving Tools:

- Taking advantage of tax-saving vehicles like pension accounts (such as the 401(k) in the United States) can allow deferring taxes on part of the income.

"It is your duty as a citizen to pay taxes; but it is not your duty to pay one penny more." - Judge Learned Hand

Practical Tips to Optimize Your Tax Situation:

1. Stay Informed:

- Stay updated on local and national tax laws. Laws can change, and your understanding must keep pace with these modifications.

2. Consult a Tax Professional:

- A professional tax consultant can offer personalized advice based on your financial situation. Investing in tax consultation can often result in significant savings.

3. Utilize Tax Breaks for Education:

- If you or your children are paying for education, explore available tax breaks, such as the tax credit for higher education.

4. Tax Planning for Retirement:

- Understand how retirement accounts work and plan accordingly. Contribute the maximum allowed to make the most of tax discounts.

5. Document Deductible Expenses:

- Keep documents and receipts for deductible expenses. This facilitates tax return preparation and can protect you in case of an audit.

Navigating the maze of tax laws may seem daunting, but knowledge is your best ally. In the next chapter, we will explore practical strategies to save money every day, further contributing to the building of your personal wealth.

Tax Deduction Optimization:

In the context of personal financial management, optimizing tax deductions is a key strategy to maximize your disposable income and reduce the tax burden. In this chapter, we will delve into how to make the most of available tax deductions.

Tax Deduction Optimization:

1. Understand Available Deductions:
 - The first and most fundamental step is to understand the tax deductions available in your country of residence. These can vary significantly and may include deductions for medical expenses, education, mortgage interest, donations, and more.

2. Keep Receipts and Documents:
 - Maintain accurate documentation of deductible expenses. Keep receipts, statements, and other relevant documents that can confirm the legitimacy of your deductions.

3. Leverage Education Deductions:
 - If you are financing higher education for yourself or your dependents, take advantage of available tax deductions. These may include tax credits for higher education or deductions for student loan interest.

4. Medical Expense Deductions:
 - Understand which medical expenses can be deducted. This may include medical expenses exceeding a certain percentage of your income, expenses for dentistry, eyeglasses, and other health-related costs.

5. Home Deductions:
 - If you are a homeowner, explore tax deductions for mortgage interest and property taxes. These can significantly reduce the tax burden associated with your home.

6. Deductions for Donations and Volunteer Work:
 - If you make donations to charitable organizations or engage in volunteer activities, you may be eligible for tax deductions. Keep accurate records of these activities and associated expenses.

7. Deductions for Self-Employed Individuals:
 - If you are self-employed, take advantage of specific deductions for this category, such as expenses for a home office, business

travel, and professional expenses.

"Every dollar you don't pay in taxes is a dollar you can invest in building your financial future." - Tony Robbins

Practical Tips for Optimizing Tax Deductions:

1. Early Planning:
   - Plan your deductions in advance. Some expenses require preparation and anticipation to be deducted correctly.

2. Consult a Tax Professional:
   - An experienced tax professional can help identify specific deductions based on your financial situation.

3. Regularly Update Your Knowledge:
   - Tax laws can change. Stay informed to make the most of new opportunities.

4. Explore Local and National Deductions:
   - Deductions can vary at both local and national levels. Explore available opportunities at both levels to maximize tax benefits.

Optimizing tax deductions requires a thorough understanding of tax laws and attention to detail.

Efficient Investments and Tax Plans:

Thoughtful investment management, coupled with intelligent tax planning, can maximize returns and reduce overall tax impact.

Efficient Investments and Tax Plans:

1. Portfolio Diversification:
   - Diversification is key to managing risk in investments. A well-diversified portfolio includes a variety of assets, such as stocks, bonds, real estate, and more. This helps mitigate the impact of market fluctuations.

2. Understand Tax Implications:
   - Each type of investment has different tax implications. Capital gains, dividends, and interest generated by each asset class are taxed differently. Understanding these dynamics allows you to optimize your tax situation.

3. Utilize Tax-Advantaged Accounts:
   - Accounts such as 401(k) or Individual Retirement Accounts (IRA) offer significant tax advantages. Contributions to these accounts may be tax-deductible or enjoy tax-deferred growth until withdrawal.

4. Explore Tax-Free Investments:
   - Some investments, like tax-exempt municipal bonds, provide

returns without the associated tax burden. Exploring such opportunities can be integral to an efficient tax strategy.

"Tax planning and investment planning are like two sides of the same coin; both must be well-balanced to achieve optimal results." - Tapan Singhel

Practical Tips for Planning Efficient Investments and Tax Plans:

1. Consult a Financial Advisor:
   - A professional financial advisor can help you develop an investment strategy aligned with your financial goals and plan your tax situation.

2. Consider Long-Term Investments:
   - Long-term investments often enjoy more favorable tax treatments compared to short-term ones. Planning for the long term can reduce the tax impact.

3. Monitor Tax Implications:
   - Before making changes to your portfolio, consider the tax implications. Selling or reallocating investments can have tax consequences that should be carefully evaluated.

4. Utilize Tax Losses:
   - Tax losses can be used to offset gains and reduce the overall tax burden. Learn to strategically use losses to optimize your tax situation.

5. Efficient Retirement Planning:
   - Invest in retirement instruments that offer tax benefits, such as pension accounts or other retirement plans. These can provide tax-free growth and benefits during retirement.

A thoughtful approach to investments, coupled with efficient tax planning, can lead to significant financial outcomes over time.

CHAPTER 9

Growth and Preservation of Wealth

The ninth chapter focuses on the creation and protection of wealth. We will explore strategies to grow your wealth over time and highlight the importance of safeguarding it from risks and unforeseen events.

Let's reflect on the wise words of Warren Buffett: "Do not save what is left after spending but spend what is left after saving."

1. Growing Your Wealth Over Time:
   - Explore strategies to grow your wealth. Thoughtful investments, consistent savings, and wealth accumulation plans are crucial for ensuring steady growth.
   - Wealth growth requires patience and discipline. Plan for the long term and maintain a holistic perspective.

2. Strategies to Protect Acquired Wealth:
   - Implement strategies to protect acquired wealth. Diversification of investments, adequate insurance, and succession plans are all crucial elements to safeguard your wealth.
   - Protecting your wealth is as important as growing it. Plan for long-term success.

3. Diversification of Investments:

- Diversify investments to ensure stable growth. Investing in a variety of assets, such as stocks, bonds, real estate, and commodities, reduces overall risk and provides opportunities for returns.

- Diversification is your defense against market uncertainty. Balance risk and reward strategically.

4. Monitor and Adjust Investment Portfolio:

- Constantly monitor and adjust your investment portfolio. Markets and economic conditions change, so ensure your portfolio aligns with your financial goals.

5. Utilize Savings and Investment Tools:

- Utilize savings and investment tools. From retirement accounts to automatic investments, leverage financial instruments that facilitate savings and wealth growth.

6. Develop a Wealth Accumulation Plan:

- Develop a wealth accumulation plan. Define clear goals, plan growth phases, and follow a well-considered strategy to accumulate wealth over time.

- A wealth accumulation plan is your roadmap to financial success. Follow it faithfully to achieve your goals.

7. Understanding the Role of Insurance in Wealth Protection:

- Understand the role of insurance in wealth protection. Life insurance, property insurance, and liability insurance can shield your wealth from unforeseen events.

- Insurance is your shield against financial surprises. Ensure your wealth is well defended.

8. Create an Estate Plan:

- Create an estate plan. Planning the transition of your wealth in an orderly manner is essential to ensure it is managed according to your wishes.

9. Minimize Inheritance Taxes:

- Minimize inheritance taxes. Understanding inheritance tax laws and implementing strategies to reduce estate taxes is vital to protect your wealth for future generations.

- "The wealth you build is meant to last. Minimize inheritance taxes to preserve your legacy." - Suze Orman

10. Practical Steps for a Smooth Wealth Transition:

- Implement practical steps for a smooth wealth transition. Clear communication, accurate documentation, and involvement of key figures ensure that your legacy is managed seamlessly.

- "A smooth wealth transition requires preparation and communication. Ensure your heirs are well-informed and prepared." - Dave Ramsey

Conclusions:

Growing your wealth requires a combination of wise investment strategies, risk management, and protection against unforeseen events. Protecting your wealth is equally important as growing it. A balanced approach that incorporates investment diversification, savings tools, and a robust protection strategy can ensure that your wealth continues to thrive over time, contributing to your financial and personal well-being.

Building Your Wealth Over Time

Growing your wealth over time requires a thoughtful approach to investments, prudent financial management, and mindful tax planning. In this chapter, we will explore practical strategies to increase your wealth over time, ensuring financial stability and long-term prosperity.

1. Diversified Investments:
    - Portfolio diversification is crucial for wealth growth. Investing in a variety of assets, such as stocks, bonds, real estate, and international markets, can help mitigate risk and maximize returns over time.

2. Long-Term Planning:
    - Adopt a long-term approach to investments. Investors who withstand short-term market fluctuations often achieve better returns over the years.

3. Contributions to Retirement Accounts:
    - Contribute the maximum allowed to retirement accounts like the 401(k) or IRA. These accounts offer significant tax benefits, including tax-free growth until withdrawal.

4. Consistent Saving Approach:
    - Maintain a consistent saving approach. Even small regular contributions can accumulate over time, contributing to the growth of your wealth.

"Money is a small house that grows when well cultivated." - Ovadia Sforno

5. Investments in Yield-Generating Assets:

- Look for investments that offer a yield, such as stocks with stable dividends. These investments can generate additional income while contributing to wealth growth.

6. Reduction of Investment Costs:

- Aim to reduce investment costs. Fees and expenses can erode your returns over time. Choose investments and platforms with competitive costs.

7. Use of Automatic Savings Tools:

- Set up automatic payments to savings or investment accounts. This ensures regular savings without having to make active decisions each time.

8. Periodic Investment Reassessment:

- Periodically reassess your investments. Your needs and goals may change over time, and your investment allocation should adapt accordingly.

"Adapt your investment strategy to your goals and personal circumstances." - Benjamin Graham

9. Continuous Investment Education:

- Invest in ongoing financial education. Understanding new opportunities and strategies can help you make more informed investment decisions.

10. Constant Expense Monitoring:

- Continuously monitor your expenses. Reducing unnecessary expenses means having more resources to invest and grow your wealth.

Conclusion:

Growing your wealth over time requires discipline, planning, and adaptability. By using a combination of smart investments, consistent saving, and thoughtful financial planning, you can build a solid foundation for your financial future. In the next chapter, we will explore practical strategies to safeguard your wealth every day, towards successful personal financial management.

Strategies to Safeguard Your Accumulated Wealth

Acquiring a significant wealth is a commendable achievement, but it is equally important to protect it. In this chapter, we will explore key strategies to safeguard your wealth against financial, legal, and unforeseen risks, ensuring enduring financial security.

1. Adequate Insurance:
   - Invest in sufficient insurance coverage to protect yourself from unforeseen events. This may include life insurance, home insurance, auto insurance, and liability insurance. Comprehensive coverage can significantly mitigate financial risks.

2. Estate Planning:
   - Implement a robust estate planning strategy. This involves creating a will, designating beneficiaries for accounts and insurance policies, and succession tax planning to reduce potential inheritance taxes.

3. Trusts and Funds:
   - Explore the use of trusts and funds to protect and transmit your wealth more efficiently. These legal structures can provide more granular control over the distribution of assets.

"A well-structured trust can be a shield against many financial challenges." - David Chilton

4. Investment Diversification:
   - Continue diversifying your portfolio. Intelligent investment distribution reduces risk and preserves your wealth against market fluctuations.

5. Asset Protection:
   - Explore options to shield your assets from potential legal actions. This may involve creating legal structures such as Limited Liability Companies (LLCs) to separate your personal assets from entrepreneurial risks.

6. Active Monitoring:
   - Actively monitor your wealth. Stay informed about financial laws and adapt your wealth protection strategy to new circumstances and opportunities.

"Constant vigilance over wealth protection is essential." - Suze

Orman

7. Debt Management:

- Keep your debt under control. Reduce unnecessary financial obligations that could undermine your wealth. Prudent debt management is an integral part of wealth protection.

8. Family Education:

- Educate your family members on financial management and wealth protection. An informed family is better equipped to preserve wealth across generations.

9. Legal and Financial Counseling:

- Seek professional legal and financial advice. A lawyer specializing in estate law and an experienced financial advisor can provide personalized advice for your situation.

10. Continuous Updates:

- Regularly update your wealth protection strategies. Changes in personal circumstances, financial laws, or market dynamics may require frequent adjustments.

Protecting wealth requires a combination of thoughtful planning, legal protection, and active management. By implementing these strategies, you can create a robust financial shield that preserves your wealth for generations to come.

Investment Diversification

Investment diversification is one of the most crucial strategies to mitigate risk and maximize returns in the long term. In this chapter, we will delve into the importance of diversification and how to implement it effectively to build a resilient and profitable portfolio.

1. Understanding Diversification:
   - Diversification is the practice of spreading your investments across a range of different assets. This can include stocks, bonds, real estate, commodities, and other financial instruments. The goal is to reduce the risk associated with a single investment class.

"Diversification is the best protection against ignorance." - Warren Buffett

2. Portfolio Risk Reduction:
   - A portfolio concentrated in a single asset class is more susceptible to market fluctuations. Diversification reduces overall risk as different assets may react differently to market conditions.

3. Geographic Diversification:
   - Consider geographic diversification. Investing in international markets can provide additional protection as economies may react differently to global events.

4. Strategic Asset Allocation:
   - Define an asset allocation strategy based on your financial

goals and risk profile. A weighted distribution among stocks, bonds, and other asset classes can contribute to achieving an optimal balance.

5. Constant Monitoring:
- Continuously monitor your diversification. Market conditions and your financial goals may change over time, necessitating adjustments to your diversification strategy.

6. Diversified Sectors:
- Within asset classes, aim to further diversify by investing in different sectors. For example, within stocks, consider shares in various sectors such as technology, healthcare, finance, and others.

7. Reinvestment of Profits:
- Reinvest profits to maintain balance in your diversification. You can do this by purchasing new assets or reallocating funds to sectors that might be underrepresented in your portfolio.

8. Periodic Adjustments:
- Periodically review and adjust your diversification based on market conditions and your evolving financial needs. Maintain flexibility to adapt to changing economic circumstances.

9. Long-Term Approach:
- Adopt a long-term approach to diversification. The strategy is most effective when implemented with a long-term perspective, ignoring short-term fluctuations.

10. Continuous Financial Education:
- Keep educating yourself about new investment opportunities and market developments. In-depth knowledge will help you make more informed diversification decisions.

Implementing an investment diversification strategy requires a thorough understanding of the financial market and your financial goals. Well-managed diversification is the key to creating a resilient portfolio capable of generating sustainable returns over time.

CHAPTER 10

Psychology of Personal Finance

The tenth chapter introduces us to the complex yet fascinating world of the psychology of personal finance. We will explore how our emotions, decisions, and mindset influence our financial choices.

Let's reflect on the insightful words of Daniel Kahneman, Nobel Prize winner in Economics: "Behavioral economics deals with how people actually make decisions, not how they should."

"The psychology of finance teaches us that how we perceive money directly impacts our financial decisions." - Dave Ramsey

1. Understanding Financial Behavior:

- Deepen your understanding of financial behavior. Recognizing how emotions, habits, and perceptions influence financial decisions is crucial for improving personal financial management.

- Your relationship with money is personal. Understanding your financial behavior is the first step to improving your financial habits.

2. Managing Emotions Related to Money:

- Learn to manage emotions related to money. Anxiety, fear, and greed can negatively influence your financial decisions. Develop strategies to maintain emotional balance in financial decision-making.

3. Addressing Financial Fear and Anxiety:

- Confront financial fear and anxiety. Identify financial fears that may hinder your decisions and develop strategies to overcome them. Financial education can be a powerful antidote to financial anxiety.

- Fear can paralyze you financially. Confront it with knowledge and awareness.

4. Recognizing and Avoiding the Herd Effect:

- Recognize and avoid the herd effect. Financial decisions influenced by mass actions can lead to undesired outcomes. Develop your decision-making autonomy and make choices based on your specific situation.

- "The herd can push you to follow the crowd even when it's not in your personal interest. Be aware and make informed choices." - Dave Ramsey

5. Understanding the Impact of Information Asymmetry:

- Understand the impact of information asymmetry. In the financial world, information is not always evenly distributed. Develop research skills and awareness to balance information asymmetry.

- In the financial world, information is power. Invest in your learning to reduce information asymmetry.

6. Preventing Impulsive Decisions:

- Prevent impulsive decisions. Choices made in the moment can lead to financial regrets. Implement strategies, such as setting rules beforehand or consulting a financial advisor, to avoid impulsive decisions.

- Impulsive decisions are often the costliest. Take control of your financial choices through planning and reflection.

7. Harnessing Technology for Financial Management:

- Leverage technology for financial management. Apps and online tools can help you monitor your finances, plan your budget, and make more informed decisions.

- Technology can be a valuable resource for maintaining financial discipline. Take advantage of it to simplify your financial management.

8. Overcoming Investment Fears:

- Overcome the fear of investments. For many people, investments can seem intimidating. Acquire knowledge and seek advice to better understand the world of investments and face fear with confidence.

9. Planning for Financial Stress Situations:

- Plan for financial stress situations. Life is unpredictable, but solid financial planning can help you face challenges without compromising your financial stability.

- "Preparation is key to dealing with financial stress. Plan for the future but be ready for the unexpected." - Suze Orman

10. Having a Financial Growth Mindset:

- Practical Example: Cultivate a financial growth mindset. Consider every challenge as an opportunity for learning and financial improvement. Resilience and determination are key to sustainable financial growth.

Conclusions:

The psychology of personal finance is a crucial element in money management. Understanding how emotions and the mind influence our financial choices can significantly enhance our ability to make informed and sustainable decisions over time. Investing in your financial awareness and developing skills to manage emotions related to money will help you create a balanced and sustainable approach to managing your personal finances.

Understanding Financial Behavior

In the complex world of personal finances, understanding one's financial behavior is crucial for making informed decisions and building a solid foundation for the future. Today, we will explore the importance of comprehending financial behavior, examining concrete examples and reflections from prominent figures in the finance world.

Looking back, we can learn from the financial psychology of figures like Daniel Kahneman and Richard Thaler, pioneers in integrating psychology into economic theories. Their work has highlighted how human behaviors, often irrational, influence financial decisions, providing a valuable learning opportunity to enhance personal financial management.

"The market is a device for transferring money from the impatient to the patient." - Warren Buffett

1. Awareness of Financial Emotions:

   - An investor might feel compelled to sell stocks during a market downturn due to the fear of losses. Understanding this emotion can help the investor make decisions based on logic rather than impulsive fear.

2. Management of Impulsivity:

- An individual might be tempted to make impulsive purchases during sales or promotions. Understanding this tendency can lead to more prudent expense management.

3. Goal-Based Planning:

- A couple might be tempted to buy a larger-than-needed house due to social influence. Understanding this desire to conform can lead to financial planning based on realistic goals.

- Social pressure can drive irrational financial choices. Planning based on one's goals and values is essential to avoid harmful external influences.

4. Realistic Risk Tolerance:

- An investor might overestimate their risk tolerance during economic growth but experience strong anxieties during market downturns. Understanding one's true risk tolerance is crucial for proper investment allocation.

- Understanding how you react under financial pressure is fundamental. Risk tolerance must be realistic to avoid detrimental decisions in critical moments.

5. Continuous Learning:

- An individual might overlook financial education, thinking decisions are too complex. Understanding the importance of continuous education can open doors to more informed financial decisions.

Conclusions:

Understanding one's financial behavior is a journey of self-awareness and continuous learning. Integrating lessons from financial psychology can improve decision-making, promote awareness of emotions, and guide towards a more balanced financial management. In the next chapter, we will explore practical strategies for managing emotions, towards successful personal financial management.

Managing Emotions and Financial Decisions

In the complex financial landscape, emotional management is crucial for making informed financial decisions and resisting market pressures. Today, we will explore the importance of managing emotions and financial decisions, tracing tangible examples and reflections from industry experts.

Reflecting on financial history, we notice how figures like Warren Buffett and Benjamin Graham have demonstrated the ability to manage emotions, staying focused on long-term strategy even during market turbulence. Their experiences teach us that emotional control is a key component of financial success.

"We are more often frightened than hurt, and we suffer more from imagination than from reality." - Seneca

1. Awareness of Financial Emotions:

   - During a market downturn, an investor might feel overwhelmed by fear and have the urge to sell stocks to avoid further losses. Awareness of this emotion can help make more rational decisions.

   - Understanding one's financial emotions is the first step towards control. Fear can lead to impulsive decisions, while rationality guides informed choices.

2. Resisting Fear and Greed:

   - During a period of strong market growth, greed might drive risky investments. Resisting this emotion and maintaining discipline is essential.

3. Long-Term Planning:

   - In response to a market downturn, a long-term investor might see an opportunity to buy undervalued stocks. Awareness of one's long-term planning can mitigate the impact of short-term fluctuations.

   - "Short-term market fluctuations are like a voting machine, but long-term they are a weighing machine." - Benjamin Graham

4. Self-Control in Spending:

- During periods of financial prosperity, the temptation to increase spending can be strong. Self-control is essential to maintain a financially sustainable lifestyle.

- Self-discipline is the bridge between goals and results.

5. Reassessing Your Risk Profile:

- After a significant change in personal financial situation, reassessing your risk profile may be necessary. Awareness of these changes can guide an appropriate reallocation of investments.

- The ability to reconsider your risk profile is a sign of financial wisdom.

6. Seeking Expert Advice in Critical Moments:

- During a period of economic uncertainty, consulting with a financial advisor can provide a clear perspective and lead to informed decisions.

- "Asking for help is not a sign of weakness, but of strength. Consulting financial experts in critical moments can make the difference between success and failure." - Robert Kiyosaki

Conclusions:

Emotional management is a critical component of financial success. Understanding and managing emotions can lead to more informed and rational decisions, promoting financial stability in the long term.

Maintaining a Positive Mindset Towards Wealth

In the overall journey of personal financial management, mindset plays a central role. Maintaining a positive mindset towards wealth is crucial for facing financial challenges with optimism and resilience. Today, we will explore the importance of this positive mindset, examining concrete examples and reflections from financial experts.

Reflecting on success stories, figures like Oprah Winfrey and Elon Musk emerge as examples of individuals who faced financial obstacles with a positive mindset. Their experiences show us that a positive mindset can be a powerful catalyst for achieving financial success.

"What we think, we become." - Buddha

"Your life will change when you change the way you look at things. From every negative, find the positive, use every failure as an opportunity for growth." - Zig Ziglar

1. Visualizing Financial Goals:

   - Clearly imagining the achievement of financial goals, such as owning a home or retiring comfortably, can fuel motivation and maintain a positive mindset.

- Visualization is a powerful motivational tool. See your financial goals already achieved in your mind and work towards them with confidence.

2. Facing Obstacles with Resilience:

- Facing financial losses or difficulties with resilience rather than despair can be crucial for overcoming obstacles and maintaining motivation.

- "Resilience is the key to overcoming financial challenges. Every failure is an opportunity to learn and grow." - Elon Musk

3. Adopting a Positive Approach to Personal Growth:

- Viewing personal growth as an investment in your financial future. Acquiring new skills and professional growth can open doors to new financial opportunities.

- "Invest in yourself. Your personal growth is the most valuable capital you have." - Jim Rohn

4. Practicing Financial Gratitude:

- Expressing gratitude for what you have financially, even in small things, can contribute to creating a positive attitude towards wealth.

5. Creating Positive Affirmations:

- Creating positive affirmations related to wealth and prosperity can positively influence your financial mindset. For example, repeating "I am worthy of financial abundance" can strengthen confidence in your ability to achieve financial success.

- Positive affirmations are like seeds you plant in your mind. Nourish them with positive actions, and you will see your wealth grow.

6. Sharing and Celebrating Financial Successes:

- Sharing and celebrating financial successes, even small ones, with friends or family can reinforce a positive mindset and fuel determination.

7. Cultivating Positive Relationships:

- Cultivating positive relationships with individuals who encourage and support your financial goals can have a significant impact on your mindset and confidence.

- "The people you surround yourself with influence your financial mindset. Seek positive relationships that inspire your path to wealth." - Robert Kiyosaki

Conclusions:

Maintaining a positive mindset towards wealth is a powerful asset in the journey towards financial success. Through visualization of goals, resilience, gratitude, and positive affirmations, you can cultivate a mindset that will guide you through challenges and lead you towards achieving your financial objectives.

CHAPTER 11

Inheritance and Succession Planning

Chapter eleven immerses us in the important world of inheritance and succession planning. We will explore strategies to ensure a smooth transition of assets, minimize estate taxes, and create a succession plan that reflects your intentions.

Let's reflect on the wisdom of Andrew Carnegie: "The man who dies rich dies in disgrace; his success often means ruin to the community."

"Planning your legacy is not just for the wealthy. It's a statement of how you want your life to have a positive impact over time." - Dave Ramsey

1. Establishing a Succession Plan:

   - Creating a succession plan means clearly outlining how you want your estate to be managed after your passing. This includes designating heirs, allocating assets, and planning for the tax aspects of the inheritance.

   - Your succession plan is your last opportunity to express how you want your estate to contribute to the greater good after your departure.

2. Minimizing Estate Taxes:

- Minimizing estate taxes is a crucial aspect of succession planning. Through strategies such as trusts, allocations, or lifetime gifts, you can reduce the tax impact on the inheritance intended for heirs.

- Preserving as much of your estate as possible for your heirs also involves understanding and optimizing the tax aspects of the inheritance.

3. Practical Steps for Ensuring a Smooth Asset Transition:

- Ensuring a smooth asset transition requires practical steps, such as creating wills, appointing executors, and maintaining accurate documentation. Involving legal professionals can facilitate this process.

- "A smooth asset transition is a lasting gift to your loved ones. Invest the necessary time to carefully plan this phase." - Suze Orman

4. Minimizing Family Conflicts:

- Succession planning must also address the management of family conflicts. Clear communication, including sharing your intentions, can reduce the risk of disputes among heirs.

5. Considering the Benefit of Charity:

- Charity can be an integral part of your succession planning. Considering donations to charitable causes can not only reduce estate taxes but also leave a lasting positive impact.

Conclusions:

Succession planning is an act of love and responsibility. Through proper planning, you can ensure that your estate is managed in accordance with your wishes, minimizing estate taxes and reducing family conflicts. Your legacy is not just a matter of figures; it is the continuation of your values and vision for the future.

Creating an Estate Plan

Creating an estate plan is an act of financial wisdom that extends beyond the present, ensuring that your estate is managed effectively and in accordance with your wishes when you are no longer able to do so. In this chapter, we will explore the importance of an estate plan, providing current examples and quotes from industry experts.

Looking at history, we can learn from the challenges faced by famous figures like Howard Hughes, the American billionaire who passed away without a clear estate plan. His post-mortem difficulties underscore the importance of accurate estate planning.

"Success is not about how much you have, but how much you can give." - Andrew Carnegie

1. Defining Estate Plan Objectives:

  - Clearly defining the objectives of the estate plan is the

first step. Whether the goal is to protect heirs, ensure business continuity, or support charitable causes, every decision should align with these objectives.

2. Will and Beneficiaries of Insurance Policies:

- A clear and updated will is fundamental. Designating beneficiaries of insurance policies must be accurate to avoid successor disputes.

- "The will is the document that tells the story of your legacy. Make sure the story is written clearly and precisely." - Warren Buffett

3. Trusts and Asset Protection:

- Trusts can offer protection and control over assets. For instance, a testamentary trust can ensure that assets are distributed according to your wishes.

4. Minimizing Estate Taxes:

- Planning to minimize estate taxes is a crucial aspect. Utilizing exemptions and tax deductions can preserve a greater value for heirs.

- Estate taxes are a reality. Thoughtful tax planning can reduce the tax impact on the estate you've worked hard to build.

5. Appointment of an Executor:

- Appointing a responsible executor can simplify the succession process. A reliable executor can ensure that wishes are carried out smoothly.

- "The executor is the guide through the maze of succession. Choosing someone trustworthy is essential for ensuring a seamless transition." - Warren Buffett

6. Open Communication with Heirs:

- Open communication with heirs is crucial. Discussing the

estate plan openly reduces the risk of misunderstandings and conflicts.

- Communication is the key to success in estate planning. Ensure that heirs understand your intentions to avoid unnecessary disputes.

7. Periodic Update of the Estate Plan:

- Life events, such as marriages, births, or financial changes, require an update of the estate plan. Keeping the plan current is essential.

- Your estate plan should grow with you. Periodic updates ensure that it is always aligned with your current goals and circumstances.

Conclusions:

Creating an estate plan is a form of care and consideration for the future of your assets and loved ones. Clearly defining objectives, planning to protect the estate, and openly communicating with heirs are key steps to ensure a seamless succession transition.

Minimizing Estate Taxes

Effective estate planning is not only about the transfer of wealth but also about minimizing estate taxes. In this chapter, we will explore the importance of reducing estate taxes, providing current examples and quotes from industry experts.

Historically, figures like John D. Rockefeller have faced challenges related to estate taxes. Their experiences highlight the need for effective strategies to protect family wealth.

1. Understanding Current Tax Laws:

- A crucial aspect is understanding current estate tax laws. For instance, comprehending exemptions and tax rates can guide estate planning decisions.

2. Utilizing Trusts to Reduce Taxes:

- The use of trusts, such as irrevocable trusts or generational trusts, can significantly reduce estate taxes. These tools allow targeted management of the estate.

- Trusts are powerful instruments for tax reduction. The right structure can safeguard the estate and minimize the tax impact.

3. Charitable Donations for Tax Deductions:

- Making charitable donations can reduce estate taxes. Some countries offer tax deductions for donations to recognized charitable organizations.

- "Donating a portion of your wealth to charitable causes is a noble way to reduce taxes and make a positive difference in society." - Warren Buffett

4. Leveraging Tax Exemptions:

- Leveraging available tax exemptions is fundamental. For

example, some jurisdictions provide exemptions for a portion of the inherited estate.

- "Tax exemptions are like golden opportunities. Knowing and leveraging available exemptions is integral to estate planning." - Suze Orman

5. Life Insurance to Cover Taxes:

- Purchasing life insurance can be a strategy to cover estate taxes. The insurance benefit can be used to pay the tax without depleting the estate.

- "It protects the family estate, providing resources to cover estate taxes."

6. Planning for the Transition of Family Businesses:

- Family businesses may benefit from specific tax advantages. Planning the transition of a business can reduce estate taxes.

- "The transition of a family business requires careful planning. The right legal structure can preserve the estate and business continuity." - Warren Buffett

7. Consultation with a Tax Expert:

- Consulting with a succession-focused tax expert is recommended. A professional can provide personalized advice based on your financial situation.

Conclusions:

Minimizing estate taxes is a key step in estate planning. With knowledge of tax laws, intelligent use of tools like trusts and life insurance, and guidance from tax experts, it's possible to reduce the tax impact on the family estate.

Practical Steps for Ensuring a Smooth Wealth Transition

Ensuring a smooth transition of wealth is an act of foresight that goes beyond mere tax reduction. In this chapter, we will explore practical steps to guarantee a seamless wealth transition, providing current examples and insights from industry experts.

Examining history, we find examples of successful and unsuccessful wealth transitions. The experiences of families like the Rothschilds and the Rockefellers offer valuable lessons on managing a wealth transition.

1. Creating Clear Legal Documents:

- Investing in the creation of clear legal documents is fundamental. The will, trusts, and directives clearly outline the wealth distribution.

2. Early Involvement of Heirs:

- Involving heirs in the planning process is essential. Initiating an open dialogue and educating heirs about financial decisions facilitates the transition.

- "Involving heirs from the start is like planting seeds for a prosperous future. Understanding and education pave the way for a successful transition." - Warren Buffett

3. Regular Assessment of Wealth:

- Regular assessment of wealth is crucial. Properties, investments, and other assets must be evaluated to ensure the estate plan reflects the current financial situation.

4. Continuous Education of Heirs:

- Continuous education of heirs is crucial. Providing educational resources and learning opportunities about financial management prepares them for the responsibility of the wealth.

- Education is the key to a successful transition. Informed heirs make wise decisions to preserve the family estate.

5. Identification of a Reliable Executor:

- Identifying a reliable executor is essential. This figure plays a crucial role in executing the will and ensuring compliance with the estate plan.

6. Consideration of Business Continuity:

- If you have a family business, considering business continuity is vital. Planning the business transition to competent heirs or establishing succession plans can preserve the business.

- "A successful transition for a family business requires detailed planning. Ensure that the business continues to thrive in the hands of future generations." - Robert Kiyosaki

7. Consultation with Industry Professionals:

- Consultation with lawyers, financial advisors, and tax experts is recommended. These professionals can offer targeted advice to optimize the transition process.

- In wealth transition, expert support is invaluable. Collaborate with industry professionals to ensure a smooth transition in compliance with current laws.

8. Contingency Planning:

- Planning for contingencies is a critical part of wealth transition. Considering unforeseen scenarios and establishing contingency plans ensures greater resilience.

- "Life is unpredictable, and succession planning must account for that. Prepare for unexpected contingencies to ensure your estate is protected in the face of surprises." - Warren Buffett

9. Creation of a Family Handbook:

- A detailed family handbook can be an excellent resource. It includes key information such as locations of important documents, contacts for professionals, and specific instructions for wealth transition.

10. Continuous Monitoring of the Process:

- Continuous monitoring of the transition process is essential. Periodic reviews of the estate plan and updates ensure that it is always aligned with your intentions and current laws.

Conclusions:

Ensuring a smooth wealth transition requires a combination of preparation, their involvement, continuous planning, and consultation with industry experts. The practical steps outlined in this chapter provide a solid guide to ensure that your wealth is managed effectively and seamlessly across generations.

CHAPTER 12

Sustaining Long-Term Financial Well-being

The twelfth chapter concludes our guide by exploring strategies to maintain a healthy financial situation in the long term. Through periodic reviews of personal finances, adapting to life changes, and continuous research and learning, we can ensure that our financial well-being thrives over time.

Let's reflect on the inspirational words of Benjamin Franklin: "An investment in knowledge pays the best interest."

1. Periodic Review of Personal Finances:

   - A periodic review of personal finances is a fundamental pillar for maintaining a healthy financial situation. Regularly revisit your budget, investments, emergency fund, and tax strategies to ensure they align with your evolving goals.

   - "Consistent review is essential to ensure your finances stay on track with your dreams and goals." - Suze Orman

2. Adapt Financial Strategy to Life Changes:

   - Life is continually evolving, and your financial strategy should adapt accordingly. Changes such as marriages, births, job transitions, or retirements require a reassessment of your finances and adjustments to the strategy.

- The ability to adapt to changes is a financial virtue. Modify your strategy when life presents new challenges and opportunities.

3. Continuous Research and Learning in Personal Finance:

- The field of personal finance is constantly evolving. Continue your research and learning about new strategies, financial instruments, and regulatory changes. Stay informed to make more informed financial decisions.

4. Maintain a Financial Growth Mindset:

- A financial growth mindset is essential for the long-term maintenance of your financial health. Consider every financial experience as an opportunity for learning and continuous improvement.

- Financial growth is a journey, not a static goal. Cultivate a mindset of continuous learning and improvement.

5. Seize Savings Opportunities:

- Savings opportunities may emerge over time. Seize opportunities, such as tax deductions, new investments, or savings options, to optimize your financial situation.

- Save wisely and take advantage of opportunities when they arise. Saved money is earned money.

6. Uphold Financial Discipline:

- Financial discipline is the key to long-term success. Maintain consistency in your financial habits, from saving to debt management, to ensure a healthy financial situation in the long term.

7. Balance the Present and the Future:

- Balance the present and the future in your financial decisions.

Plan for the future but also ensure you enjoy life today. Find a balance between saving and investing for the future and satisfying your current needs.

8. Plan for Retirement and Your Long-Term Financial Well-being:

- Retirement planning is a central element in maintaining a healthy financial situation in the long term. Ensure you have a robust retirement plan that supports your financial well-being when you reach retirement age.

- "Retirement is your reward for a lifetime of work. Plan carefully to ensure a secure and fulfilling retirement future." - Dave Ramsey

Conclusions:

Sustaining long-term financial well-being requires commitment, adaptability, and continuous learning. Through constant review, adaptation to life changes, and active research, you can ensure that your financial health continues to thrive over the years. We conclude our guide with the hope that these strategies help you build a sustainable and rewarding financial future.

Periodic Review of Personal Finances

The periodic review of personal finances is a fundamental cornerstone for long-term financial success. In this chapter, we will explore the importance of regularly monitoring and assessing your financial situation, providing current examples and quotes from industry experts.

Drawing inspiration from financial figures like Benjamin Franklin, who stated, "A well-regulated budget is an income ahead," history teaches us the importance of careful financial management.

"Ignorance of your finances is the surest way to harm your future financial security." - Dave Ramsey

1. Monitoring Income and Expenditures:

   - Monitoring income and expenditures is the first step. Use apps, spreadsheets, or online budgeting tools to accurately record all transactions.

   - "Knowing your financial situation is like navigating clear waters. Constantly monitor income and expenditures to avoid unpleasant surprises." - Warren Buffett

2. Budget Updates:

   - Budget updates are essential. Regularly reflect on your

expenses, assess changes, and update the budget accordingly to ensure precise financial planning.

3. Evaluation of Investment Performances:

- Evaluating investment performances is crucial. Regularly analyze investment returns, review asset allocations, and make changes if necessary.

- "Investments should be like a garden: they require constant attention. Evaluate performances and make adjustments to ensure sustainable growth." - Robert Kiyosaki

4. Discretionary Spending Check:

- Checking discretionary spending is important. Examine discretionary expenses, identify areas where you can save, and make conscious choices to maintain a balanced budget.

- Discretionary spending can erode your budget. Regularly analyze and cut what is non-essential to maintain financial control.

5. Review of Fees and Commissions:

- Reviewing fees and commissions is often overlooked. Examine bank charges, investment fees, and credit card fees regularly to ensure you are not paying more than necessary.

- Fees and commissions can reduce your earnings. Be vigilant in checking and seek more advantageous solutions.

6. Debt Management:

- Debt management is crucial. Regularly evaluate your debt, look for opportunities to reduce it, and establish strategies to expedite the repayment process.

- "Debt must be managed carefully. Periodic review helps you identify strategies to reduce it and achieve financial freedom more quickly." - Warren Buffett

7. Assessment of Insurance Coverage:

- Assessing insurance coverage is often neglected. Regularly check your insurance coverage to ensure it aligns with your needs and current situation.

8. Retirement Plan Updates:

- Updating retirement plans is essential. Regularly review your retirement plans, contribute as possible, and adjust the strategy based on long-term goals.

- "Retirement is your financial future. Keep your plans updated to ensure financial security when it's time to retire." - Robert Kiyosaki

9. Tax Control and Optimization:

- Tax control and optimization are crucial. Continuously seek opportunities to reduce the tax burden and maximize allowable deductions.

- Optimizing your tax situation is like an investment in yourself. Keep taxes in check and maximize deductions to retain more money in your pockets.

10. Contingency Planning:

- Contingency planning is an integral part of periodic review. Consider unforeseen scenarios like illnesses, job loss, or emergencies and assess if your resources are sufficient to handle these situations.

- In life, we cannot predict everything. Planning for contingencies ensures you are prepared to manage unexpected financial challenges.

11. Emergency Fund Creation:

- Creating an emergency fund is a critical part of financial review. Ensure your emergency fund is adequate for your current needs and update it as necessary.

- "The emergency fund is like a financial safety net. Regularly verify that it is robust enough to handle unexpected events in your life." - Warren Buffett

12. Involvement of a Financial Professional:

- Involving a financial professional is a wise move. An experienced consultant can provide an impartial perspective, assess your financial situation, and offer personalized advice.

Conclusions:

The periodic review of personal finances is a habit that pays long-term dividends. Carefully monitoring income, evaluating investment performances, updating the budget, and addressing contingencies are key steps to maintaining a solid and resilient financial management. Regularly delving into these aspects will ensure that your financial strategy is always aligned with your goals. Start implementing these review practices today to build a strong financial foundation for your future.

Adapting Financial Strategy to Life Changes

Adapting your financial strategy to life changes is essential for maintaining effective financial management over time. In this chapter, we will explore the importance of flexibility in financial decisions, providing current examples and quotes from industry experts.

Reflecting on the words of John C. Maxwell, "Wisdom is the ability to successfully adapt yesterday's strategies to today's obstacles," we can learn from history that adaptability is a valuable virtue.

"Life is a series of changes, and your financial strategy should be able to dance with it." - Robert Kiyosaki

1. Career Changes:

   - Career changes require an adjustment of the financial strategy. If transitioning to a new industry or starting a business, evaluate the financial implications and revise the budget accordingly.

   - A career is like an ever-evolving journey. Adapt your financial strategy based on the new opportunities and challenges your career may present.

2. Income Variations:

   - Income variations can occur. Whether it's a salary increase, decrease, or a change in income structure, review the budget and financial planning to reflect the new conditions.

- "Incomes can fluctuate, but your financial management should remain resilient. Adapt your financial approach to changes in your earnings." - Suze Orman

3. New Family Responsibilities:

- New family responsibilities, such as marriage or the arrival of a child, require a review of financial priorities. Update the planning to include family-related expenses and consider adequate insurance coverage.

- Family is a key element in your financial strategy. Adapt planning to ensure the safety and well-being of those you love.

4. Property Purchase:

- Property purchase is a significant financial change. Review the budget to include new expenses related to the mortgage, property taxes, and maintenance, ensuring balanced financial management.

5. Unexpected Life Events:

- Unexpected life events, such as illnesses or emergencies, may require an immediate revision of the financial strategy. Ensure you have a robust emergency fund and adjust the planning in response to these situations.

- "Life is unpredictable, and unexpected events can occur. Your financial flexibility can be the key to navigating through such challenges." - Warren Buffett

6. Regulatory and Tax Changes:

- Regulatory and tax changes can impact your finances. Stay informed about new laws and regulations and adapt your financial strategy to maximize benefits and minimize tax burdens.

7. New Investment Opportunities:

- New investment opportunities may emerge. Carefully evaluate new investment vehicles, growing sectors, and yield opportunities, adjusting your portfolio to maximize gains.

- The investment world is constantly evolving. Being open to new opportunities can enrich your financial strategy.

8. Economic Recessions:

- In times of economic recession, adapt your financial strategy to address uncertainty. Review the budget, protect investments, and seek opportunities that may arise during challenging economic phases.

- Recessions are inevitable, but your financial resilience depends on your ability to adapt to changing economic conditions.

9. Generational Transitions:

- During generational transitions, such as the wealth transfer to the next generation, adapt your financial strategy to ensure a smooth transition. Involve professionals and plan to preserve your legacy.

- Heritage succession requires careful planning. Adapt your strategy to ensure that your financial legacy is preserved during the transition.

Conclusions:

Being flexible and adapting to life changes is a crucial element in maintaining an effective financial strategy over time. Whether it's career changes, new family responsibilities, or unexpected events, your adaptability will determine your financial resilience. Stay flexible, monitor your financial conditions carefully, and adjust your strategy to successfully face challenges and capitalize on opportunities that life presents.

Continuous Research and Learning in the Field of Personal Finance

Continuous research and learning in the field of personal finance are key to maintaining effective financial management and building prosperity in the long term. In this chapter, we will explore the importance of staying informed about new financial trends, providing current examples and quotes from industry experts.

Drawing from the words of Albert Einstein, "Learning is the only soil of the mind where success can grow," we understand that continuous learning is fundamental for personal and financial development.

"Personal finances are a constantly evolving field. Staying informed is like having a compass in the financial journey." - Warren Buffett

1. Market Trends Updates:

- Stay updated on financial market trends. Study new technologies, regulatory changes, and global dynamics that could influence your investments.

- "The market is dynamic. Being aware of trends allows you to adapt your financial strategy in advance." - Suze Orman

2. Participation in Seminars and Conferences:

- Attend financial seminars and conferences. Listen to industry experts, learn new strategies, and connect with other finance enthusiasts to share knowledge.

- Conferences are an opportunity to immerse yourself in the latest financial thinking. Share and learn from those who have succeeded in the field.

3. Constant Reading of Financial Books:

- Read financial books consistently. From classic works to more recent ones, the wide range of books offers diverse perspectives that can enrich your understanding of personal finances.

- Books are an infinite source of financial knowledge.

4. Enrollment in Online Courses:

- Enroll in online courses specializing in personal finance. E-learning offers flexibility, allowing you to acquire specific skills without following a traditional path.

- Online learning is accessible to everyone. Invest time in courses that delve into specific aspects of personal finance.

5. Consultation of Reliable Financial Websites:

- Regularly consult reliable financial websites. Daily updates on financial news, expert analyses, and practical advice can provide valuable information.

- "The internet is an inexhaustible resource. Harness financial websites to stay updated on the latest developments." - Robert Kiyosaki

6. Engagement in Online Financial Communities:

- Join online financial communities. Social platforms and forums dedicated to personal finance offer opportunities for sharing experiences and mutual learning.

7. Listening to Financial Podcasts:

- Listen to financial podcasts during your commutes. Podcasts offer accessible and in-depth information on a variety of financial topics.

8. Participation in Local Discussion Groups:

- Participate in local discussion groups on finances. Connect with people in your community, exchange advice, and discover innovative approaches to financial management.

- Your local community can be an invaluable resource. Learn from those close to you.

9. Collaboration with a Financial Advisor:

- Collaborate with a financial advisor. Professional advice can offer a personalized approach to your needs and provide experience-based insights.

- "A financial advisor is like a personal mentor. Work with professionals to refine your financial strategy." - Warren Buffett

Conclusions:

Continuous research and learning in the field of personal finance are investments in yourself. By maintaining an open mindset, exploring new concepts, and adapting your strategy to new information, you can build a solid and sustainable financial foundation over time. Ongoing financial education is the key to addressing evolving challenges and capitalizing on emerging opportunities in the world of personal finance. Whether through reading, attending events, listening to experts, or interacting with online communities, every effort to broaden your knowledge will contribute to your financial success. Keep your curiosity alive, invest in your personal development, and keep learning to reach new financial heights.

Conclusions

A New Financial Beginning

The journey through "Wealth at Hand: A Quick Guide to Personal Economy" now comes to an end, but your path to mindful financial management has just begun. In this concluding chapter, we reflect on the key concepts explored in the book and embrace the opportunity for a new financial beginning.

From wise figures like Benjamin Franklin to modern visionaries like Warren Buffett, we have delved into the words of those who have shaped the financial world with wisdom and success.

"Every new day is an opportunity to improve your financial situation. Embrace the challenge and build your success." - Robert Kiyosaki

1. Reflections on the Financial Journey:

   - Take a moment to reflect on your financial journey. Have you identified clear goals, planned carefully, and adopted positive financial habits?

   - "Reflection is the key to progress. Look back with gratitude and forward with determination." - Warren Buffett

2. Implementation of Learned Strategies:

   - Implement the learned strategies. From setting financial goals to creating accurate budgets, ensure that the acquired knowledge translates into positive actions.

   - "Learning without action is like sailing without a destination. Act on what you've learned to shape your financial future." - Suze Orman

3. Adaptability to Challenges:

   - Be prepared to face challenges. Life presents obstacles, but your financial resilience is your secret weapon. Adapt your strategy, learn from difficulties, and grow.

   - "Challenges are disguised opportunities. See them as chances to grow and strengthen your financial position." - Robert Kiyosaki

4. Vision of the Financial Future:

- Visualize your financial future. Imagine the success you are building day by day. Use this vision as a guide for your daily actions.

- "Vision is the engine of success. Imagine your wealth and work consistently to make it a reality." - Warren Buffett

5. Continuous Research and Learning:

- Embrace the culture of continuous research and learning. The financial world is constantly evolving, and your commitment to learning will always keep you one step ahead.

- "Learning is an endless journey. Every new concept learned is a piece in building your financial success." - Suze Orman

6. Gratitude for the Present:

- Practice gratitude for the present. Despite challenges, recognize your current achievements and appreciate the wealth you have already built.

- "Gratitude is a powerful currency. The more you appreciate, the more you receive." - Robert Kiyosaki

7. Look to the Future with Optimism:

- Look to the future with optimism. Regardless of where you are today, tomorrow always offers the opportunity to grow, learn, and thrive.

- "Optimism is the fuel of your financial growth. Face the future with hope and confidence." - Warren Buffett

8. Invitation to a New Financial Beginning:

- Accept the invitation to a new financial beginning. Every day is a new page in the book of your financial life. Write your story with wisdom, determination, and awareness.

- "Every new beginning brings new opportunities. Embrace the future with openness and take control of your wealth." - Suze Orman

Conclusion:

The journey through "Wealth at Hand" is an important chapter in your quest for prosperous financial management. But like any good book, this ending is just the beginning of a new chapter. The acquired knowledge, formed habits, and shared wisdom will accompany you as you face the future with determination. Whether you are starting your financial journey or refining an already well-established strategy, remember that your wealth is truly within reach. With commitment, continuous learning, and resilience, you will build a financial future that reflects your vision and goals. Happy journey to financial success!

www.ingramcontent.com/pod-product-compliance
Lightning Source LLC
Chambersburg PA
CBHW071049290526
45795CB00004B/1394